COMPATIBILITY IS A MYTH

Saurabh Avasthi

Notion Press

Notion Press: USA | INDIA

Publisher:
Notion Press Media Pvt Ltd
#7, Red Cross Road,
Egmore, Chennai, Tamil Nadu 600008
Email ID: publish@notionpress.com
Phone Number: +91 44 46315631

Book Title:
COMPATIBILITY IS A MYTH

Genre: Personal Transformation, Self Help for Success
Edition: 1.0, August 2024

Language: English
Country of Origin: India
Copyright © Author: Saurabh Avasthi

Other Books by Author:

VEDIC NUMEROLOGY || ANK JYOTISH || The Proven Methodology to Accurate Prediction, 2023

The Art and Science of Signature Analysis: A Step-by-Step Guide to Deciphering Nature, Behavior, Personality and Intent, 2023

Psychology of Doodles & Scribbles: Visual Expression of the Unconscious, 2023

Encyclopedia of Graphology: A Master Practitioner's Guide - Volume I: Gestalt Method – Holistic Approach to Handwriting Analysis, 2023

Encyclopedia of Graphology: A Master Practitioner's Guide - Volume II: Trait Method – Feature Analysis Approach to Handwriting Analysis (Letters A to Z, Numerals), 2023

Basics of Graphology, 2023

Bespoke Sales Pitch: Date of Birth = Buying Behaviour = Sales Pitch, 2019

DEDICATED TO

**To my dearest parents,
I. C. Awasthi and Kiran Awasthi**

ACKNOWLEDGEMENTS

I am deeply grateful to all the individuals I have counseled whose experiences have inspired "Compatibility is a Myth." Your stories and insights into the complexities of relationships have been the driving force behind this book.

Thank you to my family and friends for their unwavering support and encouragement. Your belief in me has been invaluable.

I hope this book offers a fresh perspective on relationships, empowering you to make informed and conscious decisions. Thank you for joining me on this journey of redefining compatibility and exploring the transformative power of conscious love.

With gratitude,

Saurabh Avasthi

"Love is not about possession. Love is about appreciation."

- Osho

Index

"Opposites Attract... and Then Drive Each Other Crazy"

Prelude

The idea for this book came to me through years of personal experience in relationship counseling. In an era where astrology apps dominate our phones and "What's your sign?" has become the most asked question on dating platforms, I felt compelled to offer a fresh perspective on love, relationship, compatibility and the choices we make in our relationships.

As I sit here, pondering the countless couples I've counseled and the myriad of relationship dynamics I've observed, I can't help but think of the popular astrology app that's been making waves lately. It promises to decode your relationship with others based on the position of planets at the time of your birth. While these tools can be insightful, they often oversimplify the complex nature of human relationships.

In an era dominated by technology and instant gratification, the search for love and connection has taken a digital turn. As a relationship counselor, I've observed a staggering trend: nearly 80% of the queries on these apps revolve around love and relationships.

- "When will I find my soulmate?"
- "Is my current partner truly compatible with me?"

- "Will my relationship with my boyfriend/girlfriend lead to marriage?"

These questions echo through the digital realm, reflecting the deep-seated human desire for connection and validation. The popularity of these apps underscores a crucial point: in our fast-paced, often impersonal world, people are yearning for guidance, assurance and a sense of fulfillment in their love lives.

My background in Psychological Astrology, combined with my expertise as Advance Life Coach and my teaching experience, equips me to emphasize personal growth, self-discovery and individual responsibility in relationships.

My goal is to empower you, the reader, to take charge of your own love story, offering a holistic and transformative approach to relationships that encourages personal growth and conscious decision-making while acknowledging valuable insights.

Through countless calls, chats and in-person sessions, I've encountered the hope, anxiety and sometimes desperation in my clients' voices as they search for answers about their love lives. Many come to me after exploring compatibility tools, holding onto their reports like lifelines, seeking validation or a magical solution to their relationship challenges.

It was these interactions that inspired the idea for this book. I realized that while some apps offer interesting insights, they often oversimplify the complex nature of human relationships. They reduce love and compatibility to simplistic factors, overlooking the crucial roles of personal growth, communication and conscious choice in building lasting relationships.

The questions I frequently encounter in my practice reveal a common thread:

- "The app says we're not compatible, but we love each other. Should we break up?"
- "My soulmate's personality doesn't match mine. Will I ever find true love?"
- "The report suggests I'll meet my life partner next year. Should I avoid dating until then?"

These queries highlight a concerning trend: the outsourcing of personal responsibility and decision-making to digital algorithms and other external sources. While I respect the comfort and guidance many find in these practices, I felt compelled to offer a fresh perspective - one grounded in real-world experiences and psychological insights.

This book is born from those countless conversations, from the tears shed in my office, from the breakthroughs achieved when couples realize that their destiny isn't written in the stars but crafted by their own hands. It's a compilation of the advice I've given, the patterns I've observed and the success stories of couples who chose to look beyond zodiac compatibility to build strong, lasting relationships.

Through these pages, I aim to redefine relationship compatibility, moving away from the notion of predestined soulmates to a more empowering concept of "soul decisions" - the choices we make to love, support and grow with another person. I want to show that while astrology can offer valuable insights, true compatibility is something we build, not something we find.

My goal is to offer a balanced perspective that recognizes the appeal of guidance while highlighting the importance of personal choice and responsibility in relationships. This book is for anyone who has ever stared at their phone screen, seeking insight into their love life. It's for those who believe in soulmates and those who are skeptical. It's for anyone who wants to move beyond simplistic notions of compatibility to create deep, meaningful connections.

As we embark on this journey together, I invite you to keep an open mind. Question the narratives that apps have fed us about perfect matches and predestined love. Instead, let's explore the beautiful complexity of human connections, the growth that comes from challenges and the joy of choosing and being chosen, day after day.

This book isn't about dismissing the comfort people find in certain belief systems. Instead, it's about complementing those insights with practical wisdom, psychological understanding and real-life experiences. It's about empowering you to be the author of your own love story, guided not just by external factors, but by your values, choices and the courage to grow alongside another person.

Whether you're someone who follows these beliefs or a skeptic, whether you're single and searching or in a relationship and seeking deeper connection, this book is for you. Let's redefine compatibility, debunk the myths of perfect soulmates and discover the transformative power of conscious love.

Here are a few key points to consider as you embark on this journey:

- Relationship is something you build, not something you find.
- There are no soulmates, only soul decisions - choices we make to love, support and grow with another person.
- Your relationship is unique. What works for others may not work for you and that's okay.
- Taking responsibility for your part in the relationship is crucial for growth and happiness.

- Love is a verb. It's something you do, not just something you feel.

In the pages that follow, you'll meet couples who faced real challenges - communication breakdowns, differing life goals, external pressures and more. You'll see how they navigated these obstacles, sometimes stumbling, sometimes succeeding, but always learning.

We'll explore questions like:

- How do you maintain individuality while building a life together?
- What do you do when your partner's dreams seem to conflict with yours?
- How can you turn conflicts into opportunities for growth?
- What role does personal growth play in the success of a relationship?.

"The beginning of love is to let those we love be perfectly themselves and not to twist them to fit our own image."

- Thomas Merton

Flashback

As Arjun and Priya stood on the stage, hand in hand, they gazed out at the sea of familiar faces before them. The banquet hall was filled with friends, family and colleagues who had been part of their 25-year journey. In the front row, they could see their now-grown twins, Aarav and Asha, beaming with pride. Vikram and Ananya sat nearby, their presence a testament to the strength of forgiveness and friendship. Nisha was there too, her supportive smile reminding them of the paths not taken and the choices that led them here.

Arjun cleared his throat and began, "Twenty-five years ago, Priya and I stood before many of you, promising to love each other for better or worse. Little did we know just how much of both we'd experience."

Priya chuckled, adding, "We thought we were the perfect match, remember? Our families were so proud of finding us a '97% compatibility' through that matchmaking service."

The audience laughed, many nodding in recognition of their own similar experiences.

Arjun continued, "But life has a way of testing even the most compatible of couples. Remember our first big fight, Priya? It was over dirty dishes, of all things!"

Priya rolled her eyes playfully. "Oh yes, the Great Dish Debacle. I was working late on my startup and Arjun felt like he was doing everything at home. It was our first real lesson in communication and compromise."

"And speaking of startups," Arjun added, glancing at Vikram, "there were times when work threatened to come between us. Priya, remember those late nights at the office with Vikram? I was so jealous, convinced I was losing you to your ambitious colleague."

Vikram shifted in his seat, a mix of embarrassment and amusement on his face.

Priya squeezed Arjun's hand. "And I remember feeling lost when you started your writing career, spending hours with Nisha discussing your book ideas. But those challenges taught us the importance of trust and open communication."

Nisha nodded encouragingly from her seat, a silent acknowledgment of the role she had played in their story.

"Our journey hasn't always been smooth," Priya continued, her voice softening. "There was a time when we thought we'd lost our way completely. Do you remember, Arjun? That rainy night when we decided to separate?"

A hush fell over the room as Arjun nodded solemnly. "It was the hardest decision we ever made. We thought we were doing what was best for ourselves and for Aarav and Asha. But being apart made us realize what we truly meant to each other."

Priya's eyes glistened with unshed tears. "Those months apart were a time of incredible growth for both of us. We learned to stand on our own, to rediscover who we were as individuals. And in doing so, we found our way back to each other, stronger than ever."

Arjun smiled, looking out at their children. "Aarav, Asha, I hope you know that your mother and I didn't give up on our marriage because it was easy, but because we believed that love is a choice you make every day. We chose to fight for our family, to rebuild what we had lost."

The twins nodded, their own eyes misting over with emotion.

"And rebuild we did," Priya said proudly. "With the help of our friends," she nodded towards Dr. Meera Kapoor, their therapist, sitting quietly in the back, "and with a new understanding of what it means to be truly compatible."

Arjun chimed in, "We learned that relationship isn't about being perfect for each other. It's about growing together, supporting each other's dreams and choosing each other every day, even when it's hard."

"Especially when it's hard," Priya added with a laugh.

"Over these 25 years," Arjun continued, "we've weathered career changes, parenting challenges and personal growth. We've learned to embrace the ebb and flow of marital satisfaction, understanding that happiness is something we create together, not something that magically appears."

Priya nodded, "We've learned that love isn't just a feeling, but a series of choices. The choice to be patient when the other is struggling. The choice to celebrate each other's successes without jealousy. The choice to forgive, to trust, to keep showing up for each other day after day."

"And so, as we stand here today," Arjun said, his voice filled with emotion, "surrounded by all of you who have been part of our journey, we want to say thank you. Thank you for supporting us, for believing in us, even when we struggled to believe in ourselves."

Priya raised her glass, prompting the audience to do the same. "Here's to 25 years of love, growth and choosing each other. Here's to the challenges that made us stronger, the joys that made it all worthwhile and to all of you who have been part of our story."

"And here's to the next 25 years," Arjun added with a grin, "and whatever adventures they may bring."

As applause filled the room, Priya and Arjun shared a kiss, their love a testament to the beautiful complexity of long-term relationships. Their journey, with all its ups and downs, had brought them to this moment - not a fairy tale ending, but a real, deep, hard-won love that continued to grow with each passing day.

"Love is not something you feel. It's something you do."

- David Wilkerson

Chapter 1: A Swipe Right in the Land of Arranged Love

i. Introduction of Priya:

In the heart of Mumbai's financial district, Priya Mehta, 26, stood before a floor-to-ceiling window, her reflection a stark contrast against the city's glittering skyline. She was a vision of modern India - sharp business suit, traditional jhumkas dangling from her ears and a determined glint in her eyes that spoke volumes of her ambition.

Priya was the pride of her progressive parents - an MBA graduate from IIM Ahmedabad who had quickly climbed the corporate ladder. Her father's words echoed in her mind: "Beta, break the glass ceiling, but don't forget to use the shards to make a beautiful rangoli." This philosophy had shaped Priya into a force to be reckoned with, both in the boardroom and at family gatherings.

Her life was a carefully choreographed dance between tradition and modernity. By day, she delivered knockout presentations to CEOs; by night, she choreographed flash mobs for her cousins' sangeets. Her wardrobe told the same story - designer suits hung next to handloom sarees, each with its own purpose and tale.

ii. Priya's decision to create a profile

As Mumbai's cacophony of honking horns faded into the night, Priya found herself cross-legged on her bed, laptop balanced precariously on her knees. The glow of the screen illuminated her conflicted expression as she hovered over the "Create Profile" button on Shaadi.com.

For years, she had skillfully deflected the well-meaning but persistent inquiries about her marriage prospects. "Career first," she'd always said with a smile that brooked no argument. But now, at 26, something had shifted. Maybe it was the promotion looming on her horizon, or the wedding invitation from her younger cousin that sat on her desk like a ticking time bomb of societal expectations.

With a deep breath that felt like a surrender and a new beginning all at once, she clicked the button. As she crafted her profile, each word felt like a step into unknown territory. She wanted to project confidence without arrogance, ambition without appearing cold. It was like drafting the most important cover letter of her life - for the role of a lifetime partner.

iii. Introduction of Arjun

Meanwhile, in a cozy Bangalore apartment that smelled perpetually of filter coffee and tech dreams, the Patel family was huddled around an iPad. Mrs. Patel's fingers moved with surprising dexterity for someone who still referred to WhatsApp as "that message wala app."

"Arjun, beta! Come look at this one," she called out, her voice a mixture of excitement and exasperation. In his room, Arjun Patel, 28, pretended not to hear, his fingers flying over his keyboard as he debugged a particularly tricky piece of code.

Arjun was the epitome of the modern Indian man caught between worlds. A software engineer whose Twitter bio read "Coding karma, chai connoisseur and reluctant romantic," he found himself more comfortable with algorithms than small talk. His idea of rebellion was sneaking oat milk into his mother's sacred filter coffee when she wasn't looking.

Growing up in Bangalore, Arjun had witnessed the city's transformation from the "Garden City" to "India's Silicon Valley." He felt that transformation mirrored in himself - respecting his family's traditional values while harboring dreams that extended beyond the conventional.

iv. The Match

As Arjun finally gave in to his mother's calls and peered over her shoulder, his eyes widened imperceptibly. There on the screen was Priya's profile, her smile radiating confidence and her bio a perfect blend of wit and ambition.

"Not bad," he mumbled, trying to sound nonchalant while his heart did a little skip. For the first time, the idea of an arranged marriage didn't seem like a digital version of a cattle market.

Mrs. Patel, ever perceptive, noticed the slight change in her son's demeanor. With a knowing smile, she began the time-honored tradition of Indian matchmaking - now with a digital twist.

v. The First Meeting

Sharma Ji Chai Adda was a hole-in-the-wall establishment that had witnessed more love stories than any Bollywood director. Its peeling paint and rickety plastic chairs belied the magic that often brewed alongside its famous masala chai.

It was here that Priya and Arjun found themselves on a sunny Saturday afternoon, the aroma of cardamom and ginger mingling with the scent of nervous anticipation. Priya arrived first, her confident stride faltering slightly as she scanned the crowded stall. Arjun entered moments later, his usual tech-casual attire swapped for a crisp shirt that still bore the creases of newness.

Their eyes met and time seemed to slow. Priya's first thought was, "He's taller than his profile picture." Arjun's mind went blank except for a single notion: "Her smile is even prettier in person."

As they sat down, the rickety chairs creaking under them, an awkward silence threatened to descend. Arjun, grasping for something to say, blurted out, "So, um, do you believe in astrology?" He immediately wanted to facepalm.

But Priya, her eyes twinkling with amusement, replied, "Let's just say I check my Astro app daily but take it with a grain of sugar - or should I say, a cardamom pod?"

Just like that, the ice was broken. As they sipped their cutting chai, their conversation flowed from AI ethics to the best vada pav in Mumbai, from their favorite old Bollywood movies to the latest true-crime podcasts. They discovered a shared respect for their parents' wisdom, tempered with a burning desire to carve their own path.

In that moment, surrounded by the hustle and bustle of the chai stall, something clicked. It was like finding the perfect blend in their masala chai - spicy, sweet and unexpectedly perfect.

vi. Courtship and Wedding

What followed was a whirlwind courtship that blended the best of tradition and modernity. WhatsApp groups exploded with excitement, horoscopes were hurriedly compared (more to appease the elders than out of genuine belief) and LinkedIn profiles were scrutinized with an intensity that would put background checks to shame.

Their dates were a delightful mix of the conventional and the quirky. One day, they'd be at a posh restaurant, Priya impressively ordering wine while Arjun tried not to look too bewildered by the menu. The next, they'd be at a Comic Con, Arjun in his element explaining the intricacies of the Marvel universe while Priya nodded along, secretly googling terms under the table.

As weeks turned into months, both families grew increasingly excited. Priya's parents, progressive as they were, couldn't help but drop hints about "taking things to the next level." Arjun's mother had already started researching wedding venues, much to his embarrassment.

The proposal, when it came, was a perfect encapsulation of their relationship. Arjun had planned an elaborate rooftop dinner, complete with fairy lights and a violinist. But as he fumbled with the ring, nervous sweat making his palms slippery,

Priya simply laughed, took the ring and said, "Yes, you adorable nerd. Of course I'll marry you."

The wedding preparations were a crash course in compromise. Priya wanted a small, intimate ceremony. Arjun's family insisted on inviting what seemed like half of Bangalore. They settled on a middle ground - a big fat Indian wedding, but with personal touches that reflected their personalities.

As Priya and Arjun circled the sacred fire, their friends cheered and their families wept tears of joy. Priya's cousin, ever the dramatic one, gushed to anyone who would listen, "They're so made for each other! It's like a movie romance, but with better food and less drama!"

Little did they know, the real story - with all its spice, sweetness and occasional bitter notes - was just beginning to brew.

vii. Post-Wedding Challenges

As the last echoes of Shehnai faded and the wedding guests trickled back to their everyday lives, Priya and Arjun found themselves facing the realities of married life in modern India. The initial excitement of setting up their new home together - a sleek apartment in Mumbai's suburbs - soon gave way to the daily grind and the differences they had overlooked during their courtship began to surface.

Priya's career was on an upward trajectory. Her days grew longer, often stretching into late nights at the office. She was passionate about her work, seeing each project as a step towards breaking the glass ceiling in her male-dominated industry. When she was offered a promotion that would require extensive travel, she was ecstatic. This was what she had worked so hard for.

Arjun, while genuinely proud of Priya's achievements, struggled with the practical implications of her success. Raised in a more traditional household, he had unconsciously absorbed certain expectations about married life. He found himself grappling with feelings of neglect when Priya worked late and uncertainty about his role in their domestic life. The idea of being a "house husband" both intrigued and terrified him.

Their contrasting views came to a head one night over a dinner that had gone cold waiting for Priya to return from work. "I thought marriage meant we'd spend more time together, not less," Arjun said, his voice a mix of frustration and hurt.

Priya, exhausted from a long day, snapped back, "I thought you understood how important my career is to me. Isn't that why you chose me?"

The argument that followed was their first major one, revealing deeper insecurities and unspoken expectations on both sides. Priya felt torn between her ambitions and her desire to be a good wife, while Arjun struggled to reconcile his progressive ideals with his ingrained traditional values.

Adding to the strain was the constant pressure from family and society. Well-meaning relatives inquired about "good news" at every gathering, their eyes darting meaningfully towards Priya's midsection. Priya felt the weight of societal expectations of motherhood pressing against her career goals. Arjun, caught in the middle, tried to balance his own desire for children with supporting Priya's ambitions.

Their parents, though well-intentioned, often added fuel to the fire. Arjun's mother would casually remind Priya of her "duties as a wife," her tone sweet but her words loaded. Priya's parents, on the other hand, urged Arjun to be more "modern" in his outlook, unintentionally making him feel inadequate.

As days turned into weeks and weeks into months, Priya and Arjun found themselves at a crossroads. The fairy-tale romance of their courtship seemed like a distant memory as they grappled with the realities of merging two lives, two careers and two sets of expectations.

viii. Resolution

It was on a rare Sunday when both were home that things came to a head. Priya, frustrated with the growing distance between them, suggested they go out for chai - back to Sharma Ji Chai Adda where they first met.

Sitting on those same rickety chairs, the familiar aroma of masala chai wafting around them, they finally had the conversation they'd been avoiding. Priya spoke of her fears of losing herself in marriage, of the guilt she felt for prioritizing her career. Arjun opened up about his insecurities, his struggle to define his role in their relationship.

As they talked, really talked, for what felt like the first time in months, they realized something profound. The true test of their relationship lay not in their initial match, but in how they chose to address these challenges together.

They began to work as a team. Arjun started taking on more responsibilities at home, finding unexpected joy in mastering the perfect biryani recipe. Priya made a conscious effort to carve out quality time for them, even amidst her busy schedule. They set boundaries with their families, presenting a united front against unsolicited advice and expectations.

Their journey became a microcosm of the evolving narrative of love, career and family in a rapidly changing India. They weren't just navigating their relationship, but also the complex waters where traditional values and modern aspirations often collided and coalesced in unexpected ways.

As they walked hand in hand from the chai stall, Priya turned to Arjun with a smile. "You know, when I swiped right on that app, I never imagined it would lead to all this."

Arjun squeezed her hand, his thumb gently caressing her knuckles. He turned to face her, his eyes soft with emotion. "Me neither," he said, his voice low and tender. "But I wouldn't change a thing."

Priya felt a warmth spread through her chest at his words. She stepped closer, closing the distance between them. Her free hand reached up to cup his cheek, her fingers lightly tracing his jawline. "Neither would I," she whispered.

Their eyes locked, conveying more than words ever could. Arjun wrapped his arm around her waist, drawing her closer until their bodies were flush against each other. Priya's hand slid from his cheek to the nape of his neck, her fingers threading through his hair.

For a moment, they stood there, forehead to forehead, breathing each other in. The bustling world around them faded away, leaving just the two of them in their own little bubble of warmth and love.

Then, with a smile that crinkled the corners of his eyes, Arjun leaned in and kissed her. It was soft and sweet, full of promise and shared dreams. When they parted, both slightly breathless, Priya nestled her head in the crook of Arjun's neck, fitting perfectly as if that spot was made just for her.

As they walked away from the chai stall, they remained intertwined - Arjun's arm around Priya's shoulders, hers around his waist, their free hands clasped together.

Their love story, like the perfect cup of masala chai, had found its balance - a blend of the traditional and the modern, the sweet and the spicy, creating something uniquely their own.

ix. As months passed, this delicate balance began to shift.

As months passed, the demands of Priya's new position grew increasingly intense. Late nights at the office became the norm and business trips more frequent. Arjun found himself spending more evenings alone, the silence of their apartment a stark contrast to the lively conversations they once shared.

One night, as Priya hurriedly packed for yet another business trip, Arjun noticed a text notification on her phone. The name "Vikram" flashed on the screen, accompanied by a message that seemed oddly personal for a work colleague. Arjun's stomach churned, but he pushed the feeling aside, ashamed of his suspicion.

However, the seed of doubt had been planted. Over the next few weeks, Arjun found himself paying more attention to Priya's phone habits, noting how she'd angle the screen away from him or step out to take certain calls. The name "Vikram" appeared with increasing frequency.

Meanwhile, Priya was battling her own inner turmoil. Her new project partner, Vikram, was charming, ambitious and seemed to understand her in ways Arjun never had. Late nights working together led to shared confidences and lingering glances. Priya found herself looking forward to their interactions, guilt gnawing at her conscience.

One evening, when Priya was supposedly on a business trip, Arjun decided to surprise her by showing up at her hotel with flowers. As he approached her room, he heard laughter - Priya's laughter, mingled with a deep, masculine chuckle. His hand froze on the doorknob, heart pounding.

At that same moment, Priya was facing a pivotal decision. Vikram had just confessed his feelings for her, his hand resting on hers. The air was thick with tension and possibility. Priya felt torn between the comfort of her marriage and the excitement of this new connection.

As Arjun stood outside the door, grappling with whether to confront what he feared or walk away and Priya teetered on the brink of a decision that could shatter her marriage, both found themselves at a crossroads. The trust they had built, the love they had nurtured - everything hung in the balance.

The next move would determine the course of their relationship. Would Arjun open the door? Would Priya cross a line she couldn't uncross? Or would they find their way back to each other, stronger for having faced this test?

As Priya's career soared, Arjun found himself grappling with a growing sense of inadequacy. His own job, once a source of pride, now felt mundane in comparison to Priya's high-flying corporate world. The long hours she spent at work left him feeling increasingly isolated and overlooked.

One evening, while mindlessly scrolling through social media, Arjun received a message from Nisha, an old college friend. Their casual catch-up quickly became a daily ritual, with Arjun finding solace in Nisha's understanding and attention. She seemed to appreciate him in ways he felt Priya no longer did.

As weeks passed, Arjun found himself sharing more with Nisha than with Priya. He confided his frustrations, his dreams and his fears. Nisha's responses were always supportive, peppered with flirtatious undertones that Arjun pretended not to notice - or perhaps secretly enjoyed.

One particularly lonely night, after Priya canceled their dinner plans for a last-minute work emergency, Arjun agreed to meet Nisha for a drink. It was supposed to be innocent - just two friends catching up. But as the evening progressed and the drinks flowed, the line between friendship and something more began to blur.

Nisha's hand lingered on his arm, her laughter at his jokes seemed more intimate and Arjun felt a long-forgotten spark of excitement. As they stood outside the bar, saying goodbye, there was a moment of electric tension. Nisha leaned in, her intention clear.

In that split second, Arjun's mind raced. He thought of Priya, of their marriage, of the promises they'd made. But he also thought of the loneliness, the neglect he'd been feeling. His heart pounded as he stood on the precipice of a decision that could change everything.

Meanwhile, across town, Priya was rushing home, eager to surprise Arjun with the news of a promotion that would allow her to spend more time at home. She clutched a bottle of champagne, her heart full of plans to reconnect with her husband.

As Priya approached their apartment and Arjun stood frozen in that moment with Nisha, the future of their marriage hung in the balance. Would Arjun step back from the brink, or would he succumb to the temptation before him? And how would Priya react if she discovered this hidden chapter in their life story?

———

"Love is
like a fart.
If you have
to force it,
it's
probably
crap."

Author's Insight

Attraction between individuals typically falls into two broad categories: similarity and complementarity. In the first category, people are drawn to those who share their interests, such as common topics of discussion, food preferences, or life philosophies. This similarity fosters companionship and a desire to spend time together, often resulting in close friendships that reinforce mutual interests.

The second category involves attraction to opposite traits. Here, individuals seek qualities they lack in themselves. For instance, an introvert might be drawn to an extrovert, or a timid person to someone bold and assertive. This attraction stems from a desire for completeness, where one partner's strengths compensate for the other's weaknesses.

Another factor in attraction is the subconscious comparison to idealized figures. People often develop mental images of their ideal partner based on admired traits observed in parents, close relatives, or other influential figures during their formative years. These ideals, while not always consciously acknowledged, profoundly influence partner selection and relationship dynamics.

When reality fails to match these subconscious expectations, it can lead to tension. Individuals may find themselves automatically comparing their partners to these idealized figures, often without realizing it. This subtle comparison process can trigger conflicts, manifesting as verbal or physical outbursts when discrepancies become too pronounced.

This phenomenon extends to various aspects of life, including daily interactions, professional settings and intimate relationships. In the early stages of a partnership, one person may attempt to mold the other's behavior to align with their internalized ideal.

It is at this juncture that relationship problems often begin. Initially, partners may try to "adjust" or "compromise" to maintain harmony. However, these terms carry negative connotations and should be avoided. Instead, the focus should be on acceptance - embracing both the positive and negative aspects of one's partner without attempting to change them fundamentally.

True behavioral change is a gradual process that occurs naturally as the relationship evolves. By prioritizing acceptance over modification, couples can build a stronger, more authentic connection based on mutual understanding and appreciation of each other's unique qualities.

Priya and Arjun's relationship faced challenges common to many couples, including career pressures, unmet expectations and external temptations. However, they made a crucial decision to confront their issues directly, choosing open communication and teamwork to overcome their difficulties. By prioritizing their relationship, setting boundaries with family and supporting each other's growth, they successfully blended traditional values with modern aspirations. This helped them avoid common pitfalls such as neglecting their partnership for career advancement, succumbing to external pressures, or seeking validation outside the relationship. This illustrates how conscious choices and open dialogue can strengthen a bond, leading to a more balanced and fulfilling partnership, even when faced with significant challenges.

Byrne's Attraction-Similarity Hypothesis suggests that individuals tend to be drawn to others who exhibit comparable attitudes, beliefs and values. While Byrne's work primarily focuses on the similarity aspect of attraction, it's worth noting that subsequent research has also explored the complementarity theory, supporting the idea that opposites can indeed attract in certain circumstances.

"We're perfectly compatible - we both think the other one needs to change."

Chapter 2: The Illusion of Compatibility

As the Mumbai skyline twinkled in the distance, Priya stood at the window of her hotel room, her reflection a ghostly overlay on the city lights. The weight of her decision pressed heavily on her shoulders. Behind her, Vikram waited, his presence both alluring and terrifying.

"Priya," Vikram's voice was soft, enticing. "We both know there's something here. Something your algorithm-approved husband could never understand."

His words struck a chord. Priya thought back to that moment when she first saw Arjun's profile, the excitement of finding someone who seemed so perfectly compatible. But now, standing here with Vikram, she wondered if that compatibility was just an illusion, a mirage in the desert of modern relationships.

Meanwhile, across the city, Arjun found himself caught in Nisha's magnetic gaze. The bar's neon lights cast a surreal glow, making everything feel dreamlike and disconnected from reality.

"Arjun," Nisha whispered, her lips inches from his. "Remember how we used to talk about soulmates in college? Maybe the universe has a different plan for us."

Arjun's mind raced. He thought of Priya, of their carefully curated compatibility, of all the boxes they had ticked off on their matching algorithms. But standing here with Nisha, he felt a spark that defied all logical relationship metrics.

In that moment, both Priya and Arjun faced the same realization: compatibility wasn't a guarantee of happiness or fulfillment. It wasn't about matching interests or aligning life goals. It was something more intangible, more volatile.

Priya took a step back from Vikram, her hand reaching for her phone. Arjun gently pushed Nisha away, his fingers tracing the outline of his wedding ring.

As if guided by some cosmic force, they both typed out the same message: "We need to talk. Meet me at Sharma Ji Chai Adda."

The familiar chai stall, with its peeling paint and rickety chairs, seemed like a sanctuary in the chaos of their emotions. As Priya and Arjun approached from opposite directions, they saw each other and stopped, the weight of their almost-transgressions heavy between them.

They sat down, the same chairs creaking under them as they had on their first meeting. The aroma of cardamom and ginger swirled around them, a reminder of simpler times.

"I thought we were perfect for each other," Priya began, her voice barely above a whisper.

"I did too," Arjun replied, his eyes meeting hers. "But maybe that's the problem. We believed in the illusion of perfect compatibility."

As they talked, really talked, for what felt like the first time in months, they realized something profound. True relationships weren't about matching profiles or shared interests. It was about choosing each other, every day, through the ups and downs. It was about growing together, challenging each other and sometimes, forgiving each other.

They shared their temptations, their fears and their disappointments. There were tears, accusations and moments of painful silence. But there was also honesty, vulnerability and a rekindling of the connection that had brought them together in the first place.

As the night deepened and the chai stall owner began stacking chairs around them, Priya and Arjun reached a new understanding. They realized that their journey wasn't about finding a perfect match, but about building a relationship that could withstand the imperfections of reality.

"So where do we go from here?" Arjun asked, reaching for Priya's hand across the table.

Priya intertwined her fingers with his, a small smile playing on her lips. "We stop chasing the illusion of a perfect relationship and start creating our own reality. Together."

As they walked home, hand in hand, they knew that their challenges were far from over. The ghosts of Vikram and Nisha would linger, a reminder of the fragility of perceived relationship. But they also knew that they were choosing each other, not because an algorithm said they were perfect, but because they were willing to work through the imperfections.

—

"Happily Ever After: A Fairy Tale Best Left in Books"

Author's Insight

In the routine of daily life, it's natural for couples to begin taking each other for granted, overlooking small but crucial aspects of communication. The cornerstone of effective communication is, undoubtedly, listening.

How often do we find ourselves formulating responses before our partner has finished speaking, as if we can predict their thoughts? This tendency is especially pronounced with those closest to us. We interrupt, assuming we know what they'll say next, rather than truly hearing them out.

This behavior leads to a widening communication gap. As this chasm grows, individuals may seek validation and understanding outside their relationship. It's only natural that the attentive ear we lend to outsiders - a courtesy we've neglected to extend to our partners - can become the genesis of new attractions or affinities.

These seemingly innocuous acts of lending an ear to others can be the first steps toward emotional distance in a relationship. If not addressed promptly, they can escalate into more significant issues.

Sometimes, the most important thing we can do is simply listen. Often, our partner merely wants to be heard and understood, without immediate judgment or response.

Priya and Arjun illustrate both the pitfalls and the power of honest dialogue. They teetered on the brink of infidelity, tempted by Vikram and Nisha due to poor communication and neglect in their marriage. However, they made the crucial decision to confront their issues head-on, meeting at the place where their relationship began. By openly sharing their temptations and fears, they demonstrated vulnerability and a commitment to working through their problems together. This choice to prioritize their relationship over fleeting attractions and to reconnect through open communication ultimately strengthened their bond. This highlights common mistakes couples make, such as believing in perfect compatibility and seeking validation outside the relationship instead of addressing internal issues.

Dr. John Gottman's "Four Horsemen of the Apocalypse" theory suggests that couples who regularly engage in the negative communication patterns are more likely to experience relationship dissatisfaction and, ultimately, divorce. Conversely, couples who practice active listening, show appreciation and respond to each other's emotional needs are more likely to have stable, satisfying relationships.

"A great marriage is not when the 'perfect couple' comes together. It is when an imperfect couple learns to enjoy their differences."

- Dave Meurer

Chapter 3: The Chemistry of Connection

As Priya and Arjun walked home from Sharma Ji Chai Adda, the first light of dawn painting the Mumbai sky, they couldn't help but reflect on the journey that had brought them together - and nearly torn them apart.

Dr. Aisha Khan, a renowned neuroscientist and Priya's college roommate, had always been fascinated by the couple's relationship. She invited them to participate in a study on the science of attraction at her lab in the prestigious Tata Institute of Fundamental Research.

"You two are a perfect case study," Aisha explained as she attached electrodes to their temples. "An arranged marriage that seemed to defy the odds, until it didn't. I want to understand what's happening in your brains."

As Priya and Arjun viewed photos of each other, their initial meeting and their wedding day, their brains lit up with activity. Aisha observed the flood of oxytocin, dopamine and serotonin - the chemical cocktail of love and bonding.

"Fascinating," Aisha murmured. "Your brains are responding as strongly now as they likely did when you first met. But let's dig deeper."

She then showed them photos of Vikram and Nisha. To their surprise - and slight embarrassment - Priya and Arjun's brains showed similar patterns of activation.

"Don't be ashamed," Aisha reassured them. "Attraction is largely biological. What matters is what we choose to do with those feelings."

As they left the lab, Priya and Arjun encountered Vikram in the lobby. He was there for a different study, but the tension was palpable. Arjun felt a surge of jealousy, his body flooding with cortisol and adrenaline - the stress hormones.

Meanwhile, across town, Nisha was having lunch with her best friend, Zara, a cultural anthropologist.

"I can't stop thinking about Arjun," Nisha confessed. "We have such a strong connection."

Zara listened thoughtfully. "You know, in many cultures, the concept of a soulmate or perfect match is deeply ingrained. But it's largely a social construct. In some societies, love is expected to grow after marriage, not before."

As Nisha pondered this, her phone buzzed with a message from Arjun: "I enjoyed catching up, but I need to focus on my marriage. Take care."

Nisha felt a pang of disappointment, but also a sense of respect for Arjun's decision.

Back at home, Priya and Arjun decided to seek help from Dr. Rajesh Sharma, a couples therapist known for his innovative approach combining Western psychology with Eastern philosophy.

"Tell me," Dr. Sharma began, "what drew you to each other initially?"

Priya smiled, remembering. "Arjun's kindness and his quiet confidence. It was so different from the aggressive ambition I was used to in my corporate world."

Arjun nodded. "And I was captivated by Priya's passion and drive. She inspired me to dream bigger."

Dr. Sharma leaned forward. "And what about Vikram and Nisha? What attracted you to them?"

The couple shifted uncomfortably, but Dr. Sharma encouraged their honesty.

"Vikram understood my career ambitions in a way I thought Arjun never could," Priya admitted.

"And Nisha made me feel valued and heard when I was feeling neglected," Arjun added.

Dr. Sharma nodded. "Often, we're attracted to people who fulfill unmet needs or represent parts of ourselves we've neglected. The key is to recognize these needs and work on them together."

Over the next few weeks, Priya and Arjun embarked on a journey of rediscovery. They took a DNA compatibility test, more out of curiosity than conviction and laughed at the pseudo-scientific results that claimed they were a "97% match."

They attended a workshop on love languages, realizing that Priya felt love through acts of service, while Arjun valued quality time above all. This insight helped them bridge many of their misunderstandings.

One evening, they bumped into Vikram and his wife, Ananya, at a cultural festival. The initial awkwardness gave way to a surprisingly pleasant conversation. Ananya, an artist, invited them to her gallery opening the following week.

At the gallery, surrounded by Ananya's vibrant paintings depicting the complexities of modern Indian relationships, Priya and Arjun found themselves in a deep discussion with Vikram and

Ananya about the challenges of balancing career, marriage and societal expectations.

"You know," Ananya mused, "in my art, I try to capture the beautiful mess of human connections. There's no perfect compatibility, just perfectly imperfect moments."

As they left the gallery, hand in hand, Priya turned to Arjun. "You know, I'm glad we didn't give up on us. This journey, with all its ups and downs, is ours. And I wouldn't have it any other way."

Arjun squeezed her hand, a warmth spreading through his chest. "Neither would I, Priya. Neither would I."

—

Author's Insight

What Could Have Gone Wrong:

Priya and Arjun could have allowed their attractions to Vikram and Nisha to destroy their marriage. They might have mistaken initial chemistry for lasting compatibility, or given up on their relationship due to challenges and unmet needs.

What They Did Right:

They chose to confront their issues honestly, sought professional help and committed to understanding each other better. They participated in scientific studies and workshops to gain insights into their relationship dynamics.

Choices Made and Their Results:

By choosing to work on their relationship, understand their needs and communicate openly, Priya and Arjun strengthened their bond. Their decision to face their attractions to others head-on and refocus on each other led to a deeper, more authentic connection.

Common Mistakes Couples Make:

Many couples mistake initial attraction for lasting compatibility, neglect to address unmet needs within the relationship, or fail to adapt and grow together. Priya and Arjun's story highlights the importance of continuous effort, communication and mutual growth in maintaining a strong relationship.

Dr. Helen Fisher's studies on the brain in love reveal that long-term couples who report still being in love show similar brain activity to those newly in love, mirroring Priya and Arjun's brain scans.

Research on the Michelangelo phenomenon by Dr. Caryl Rusbult shows that individuals who support their partner's ideal self have happier and more stable relationships.

"You are not Made for Each Other, You Make for Each Other"

Chapter 4: The Alchemy of Love

As the Mumbai monsoon pelted their apartment windows, Priya and Arjun found themselves in a familiar embrace on their balcony, watching the rain transform the city. Five years had passed since their moment of truth at Sharma Ji Chai Adda and life had taken them on an unexpected journey.

"Remember when we thought we were perfectly compatible?" Priya mused, her fingers tracing lazy circles on Arjun's chest.

Arjun chuckled, pulling her closer. "Oh yes, our '97% match' according to that ridiculous DNA test. If only it were that simple."

Their laughter was interrupted by a cry from inside. "Speaking of complications," Arjun sighed, reluctantly untangling himself from Priya.

They entered the nursery where their twins, Aarav and Asha, were awake and demanding attention. As they tended to their 18-month-old children, Priya and Arjun exchanged a look that spoke volumes - exhaustion, joy, frustration and deep love, all rolled into one.

The arrival of the twins had been both a blessing and a challenge. Priya had struggled with the decision to step back from her high-powered career, while Arjun had surprised everyone (including himself) by thriving in his role as a hands-on father.

"You know," Priya said as she rocked Asha back to sleep, "I used to think being 'made for each other' meant everything would just fall into place. But look at us now - we're definitely 'making for each other' every single day."

Arjun nodded, gently placing a sleeping Aarav in his crib. "It's not always easy, but I wouldn't have it any other way."

The next morning, as they prepared for their annual double date with Vikram and Ananya, Priya found herself lost in thought. The four of them had formed an unlikely friendship, bonded by their shared experiences of navigating modern relationships.

At the trendy fusion restaurant, conversation flowed easily, punctuated by laughter and knowing glances. As they savored their molecular gastronomy creations, Ananya broached a subject that had been on her mind.

"So, Vikram and I have been thinking about having a baby," she said, a mix of excitement and apprehension in her voice.

Priya and Arjun exchanged a look, remembering their own journey to parenthood. "It's amazing," Priya began, "but it will test your relationship in ways you never imagined."

Vikram leaned forward, curious. "How so? You two always seem to have it all together."

Arjun laughed, a hint of irony in his voice. "Oh, if you only knew. Remember when we thought we were the perfect match, Priya?"

Priya nodded, a wry smile playing on her lips. "We've learned that there's no such thing as a perfect partner or a perfect match. It's about growing together, adapting and sometimes, completely reinventing yourselves."

As the night wore on, the conversation deepened. They discussed the challenges of maintaining passion in long-term relationships, the constant negotiation of roles and expectations and the societal pressures they all faced.

"You know," Arjun mused, his hand finding Priya's under the table, "I think the whole idea of compatibility is a journey, not a destination. We're constantly evolving, individually and as a couple."

Priya squeezed his hand, feeling a rush of warmth. "Exactly. Every day, we choose each other. We work on our relationship, we compromise, we argue, we make up. It's not always pretty, but it's real."

Later that night, as Priya and Arjun lay in bed, the soft sounds of their sleeping children coming through the baby monitor, they found themselves in a tender moment of connection.

"You know," Priya whispered, her lips brushing against Arjun's ear, "I think I love you more now than I did when we first got married."

Arjun turned to face her, his eyes dark with desire. "Is that so? And why is that, Mrs. Patel?"

Priya's hand trailed down his chest, her touch igniting sparks between them. "Because now I know you - really know you. All your flaws, all your strengths. And you know me, really know me. It's not about being perfect for each other, it's about being real with each other."

Their lips met in a passionate kiss, years of shared experiences and deep understanding fueling their desire. As they made love, it was with a intensity born not just of physical attraction, but of a profound emotional and intellectual connection that had been forged through challenges and triumphs.

In the afterglow, as they lay entwined, Arjun mused, "You know, if someone had told me on our wedding day that this is where we'd end up, I wouldn't have believed them."

Priya propped herself up on an elbow, looking at him curiously. "What do you mean?"

"Well," Arjun said, his fingers tracing lazy patterns on her back, "I thought I was marrying this perfect woman who would complete me. But instead, I got a real woman who challenges me, frustrates me sometimes, but ultimately makes me a better person. And together, we're creating something far more beautiful and complex than I ever imagined."

Priya smiled, leaning down to kiss him softly. "I couldn't have said it better myself. We're not made for each other, we're making for each other. Every single day."

As they drifted off to sleep, wrapped in each other's arms, they both knew that tomorrow would bring new challenges, new negotiations, new moments of joy and frustration.

———

Author's Insight

Parenthood marks a pivotal and challenging phase in any relationship. The arrival of a new family member brings an influx of responsibilities, a significant increase in workload and a complete transformation of lifestyle. Modern parenting has evolved dramatically, differing substantially from earlier generations in both child-rearing approaches and the distribution of parental duties.

With the trend of delayed marriages, couples often find themselves starting families later in life. This timing frequently coincides with critical career stages, forcing parents to carefully balance their professional aspirations with familial obligations. To navigate this demanding period successfully, couples must prioritize effectively, share responsibilities equitably and seek support when necessary.

The art of parenting itself has become increasingly complex in the modern era. Contemporary child-rearing practices are vastly different from those of previous generations, reflecting the rapid changes in society, technology and cultural norms. Parents today face the challenge of raising children in an environment that bears little resemblance to their own upbringing. The current generation of children, along with the unique circumstances they face, requires a fresh approach to parenting - one that acknowledges and adapts to the complexities of the modern world.

Priya and Arjun could have struggled with the dramatic lifestyle changes brought by parenthood, particularly given their later start in life and established careers. The demands of raising twins might have strained their relationship, leading to resentment over division of responsibilities. The couple adapted to their new roles, with Arjun embracing hands-on fatherhood and Priya navigating career adjustments.By choosing to view their relationship as an evolving journey rather than a fixed state, they strengthened their bond amidst the demands of parenting. Many struggle to balance career aspirations with familial obligations, fail to adapt parenting styles to modern needs, or neglect their relationship amid the pressures of child-rearing. Some may also resist seeking necessary support or fail to equitably share parental duties, issues that Priya and Arjun seem to have navigated successfully.

The "Becoming Parents Study" conducted by John and Julie Gottman reveals that most couples experience a decline in relationship satisfaction after having a child, highlighting the significant impact of parenthood.

"You can't start the next chapter of your life if you keep re-reading the last one."

Chapter 5: Unspoken Histories

As Priya and Arjun lay in bed, a comfortable silence enveloped them. The soft patter of rain against the window brought a flood of memories to Priya. Her mind wandered to her college days, to a time she had never shared with Arjun.

Priya's thoughts drifted to Rohit, her first real crush at IIM Ahmedabad. She could almost smell the musty scent of old books in the library where they'd spent countless hours studying together. Rohit had been brilliant, ambitious, devastatingly handsome - everything she thought she wanted back then.

She remembered the late-night debates, the stolen glances across the cafeteria, the rush of their first kiss behind the economics building. It had been exhilarating, but looking back, Priya realized how superficial it all was. They had looked perfect on paper, but there had been no real depth to their connection.

A small smile played on Priya's lips as she thought about how different her relationship with Arjun was. With Rohit, she had been in love with an idea, a projection. With Arjun, she was in love with a real, complex human being.

Beside her, unaware of Priya's inner monologue, Arjun was lost in his own reminiscence. His mind wandered to Anjali, the girl he had matched with on Tinder in his second year of engineering. He recalled the excitement of their first match, the butterflies in his stomach as they planned their first date.

Arjun suppressed a chuckle, remembering how obsessed they had been with curating the perfect social media presence. Every date had been an opportunity for an Instagram post, every shared interest a chance to showcase their 'perfect' compatibility. But behind the filters and carefully crafted captions, there had been an emptiness, a lack of genuine connection that he hadn't recognized at the time.

His hand found Priya's in the darkness and he marveled at how different this felt. With Priya, there was no need for pretense. Their relationship wasn't perfect, but it was real and that made all the difference.

As Arjun's thumb traced lazy circles on Priya's palm, his mind drifted to a memory he had never shared with anyone. In his final year, he had matched with a girl on OhMyMatch who had seemed perfect. Their late-night chats had been filled with laughter and deep conversations. He had felt understood in a way he never had before.

Arjun's heart raced as he recalled the day they were supposed to meet. He had arrived at the cafe, his palms sweaty with anticipation. And then he had seen her - Jaya. She had been even more beautiful in person, but she hadn't been there to meet him. She had been waiting for someone named Anand..

Lying next to Priya now, Arjun marveled at the twist of fate. He had walked away that day, never revealing his presence, thinking he had missed his chance at something special. Little did he know that years later, an arranged marriage setup would bring them together.

Priya, oblivious to Arjun's thoughts, was remembering her own experience with OhMyMatch. She recalled the excitement of matching with someone who seemed perfect on paper, the nervousness as she sat in that cafe waiting for Rohan to show up. He never did and she had left feeling disappointed and disillusioned with the whole idea of app-based dating.

As they lay there, lost in their own thoughts, Priya and Arjun were unknowingly reflecting on the same themes - the illusions of perfect compatibility, the role of perception and expectations in shaping relationships and the fear of missing out that had driven their dating experiences in college.

Priya turned to face Arjun, studying his profile in the dim light. She felt a rush of affection for this man who had surpassed all her expectations, who challenged her perceptions daily, who had turned out to be so much more than any algorithm could have predicted.

Arjun, feeling Priya's gaze, turned to meet her eyes. In that moment, without words, they both felt a deep appreciation for the journey that had brought them together. All the missteps, the near-misses, the lessons learned - they had all led to this moment, to this love that was real, complex and infinitely more satisfying than any idealized version they had chased in their youth.

As they moved closer, their bodies fitting together with the familiarity of long-time lovers, they both silently acknowledged the unspoken histories that had shaped them. Their lips met in a kiss that was both tender and passionate, a testament to the depth of their connection.

In the quiet of their bedroom, as rain continued to fall outside, Priya and Arjun reaffirmed their choice - not of a perfect partner, but of a real one. A choice they made every day, with full awareness of each other's flaws and strengths, complexities and contradictions. And in that choice, they found a love far more profound than anything they could have imagined in their college days.

—

Author's Insight

Should couples have secrets from each other? This is a common and crucial question that many couples grapple with in their relationships. The answer, perhaps surprisingly to some, is yes - it's perfectly acceptable for couples to have secrets. It's not necessary, nor always beneficial, to share every minute detail of one's life with a partner. Everyone, regardless of their relationship status, has a right to personal privacy and individual experiences.

The real issue often lies not in keeping a secret itself, but in the guilt associated with doing so. In many relationships, one partner tends to be more expressive, sharing even the smallest details of their day-to-day life. This can inadvertently put pressure on the more reserved partner, who may then feel guilty for not being equally forthcoming. This guilt is misplaced and potentially harmful to the relationship.

It's important to recognize that guilt, especially in this context, can be detrimental to personal well-being and relationship dynamics. It's one of the most potent negative emotions, capable of eroding self-esteem and creating unnecessary tension between partners. The silent partner should not feel obligated to match their more expressive counterpart in terms of sharing every detail.

What's crucial is maintaining trust and open communication in the relationship. This doesn't mean divulging every secret, but rather being honest about one's need for privacy when necessary. Partners should respect each other's boundaries and understand that having personal space doesn't equate to a lack of love or commitment.

Moreover, it's essential to differentiate between harmless personal secrets and information that could significantly impact the relationship. While it's okay to keep some things private, withholding information that directly affects your partner or your relationship can be detrimental and may breach the trust between you.

Couples should strive for a balance between openness and personal privacy. It's healthy to have some secrets, as long as they don't undermine the foundation of trust in the relationship. Remember, what's past is past - dwelling on guilt over keeping harmless secrets is unproductive and unnecessary. Instead, focus on fostering a relationship built on mutual respect, understanding and trust.

Priya and Arjun harbored memories of past romantic experiences that they hadn't shared with each other, yet these secrets didn't undermine their connection. They demonstrated a balance between openness and personal privacy, maintaining individual experiences while fostering a strong bond based on mutual understanding and respect. Priya and Arjun's reflections on their past experiences actually deepened their appreciation for each other, showing that selective privacy can sometimes enhance a relationship rather than harm it. It is important to differentiate between harmless personal secrets and information that could affect the partnership, emphasizing that the key lies in maintaining trust while respecting each other's boundaries and right to personal space.

Dr. Beth Easterling's 2012 study, "I'm Hiding It: Forms of Information Concealment in Close Relationships," published in the Journal of Social and Personal Relationships, offers empirical support for the concept of healthy secrecy in relationships. This research found that keeping some information private is common and normal, with 92% of participants reporting concealment of information from their partners at some point. The study identified various types of secrets, including those related to prior relationships, personal habits and finances and explored motivations for secrecy such as protecting a partner's feelings or maintaining privacy. Importantly, the research suggested that some level of information concealment did not necessarily harm relationship satisfaction and could sometimes contribute to relationship stability.

"Acceptance Not Expectance, is the key to everlasting relationships"

Chapter 6: Building Successful Relationships

The morning sun filtered through the curtains, casting a warm glow on Priya's face as she stirred awake. She reached for her phone, a habit she'd been trying to break and saw an email that made her heart race. Her startup had just secured a major investor.

Excitedly, she turned to Arjun, who was still sleeping peacefully. "Arjun! Wake up! I have amazing news!"

Arjun blinked groggily, a smile forming on his face as he saw Priya's excitement. "What is it, love?"

As Priya shared her news, she noticed a flicker of something in Arjun's eyes. Pride? Concern? She couldn't quite place it.

"That's wonderful, Priya," Arjun said, pulling her into a hug. "I'm so proud of you."

But as the days passed, Priya sensed a growing tension. Arjun's smiles seemed forced, his questions about her work perfunctory. One evening, as they sat on their balcony, the twins asleep inside, Priya decided to confront the elephant in the room.

"Arjun, what's really bothering you about my startup's success?"

Arjun sighed, running a hand through his hair. "It's not that I'm not happy for you, Priya. I am. It's just... I guess I always expected that once we had kids, you'd want to slow down. To be here more."

Priya felt a surge of anger, quickly followed by hurt. "So you expected me to give up my dreams? To be content with just being a mother?"

"No! That's not what I meant," Arjun backpedaled. "I just... I guess I had this expectation of what our family life would look like. And now, with your startup taking off, it feels like everything's changing."

As they talked late into the night, they realized how their unspoken expectations had been shaping their reactions. Arjun had to confront his traditional views of family roles, while Priya had to acknowledge her fear of losing her identity to motherhood.

"I love our family, Arjun," Priya said softly. "But I also love my work. It's part of who I am. Can you accept that?"

Arjun took her hand, his eyes meeting hers. "I'm trying, Priya. I really am. I think... I think I need to let go of my expectations and really see you - all of you."

As weeks turned into months, Priya and Arjun found themselves navigating a new normal. Priya's startup demanded more of her time, while Arjun took on more responsibilities at home. It was a delicate balance and some days felt like a constant struggle.

One particularly challenging day, Arjun found himself alone with the twins, both running a fever. He'd had to cancel an important meeting at work and as he tried to soothe Aarav's cries while keeping an eye on Asha, he felt overwhelmed.

When Priya returned home late that night, she found Arjun sitting on the kitchen floor, surrounded by scattered toys and half-eaten meals.

"I can't do this, Priya," he said, his voice cracking. "I'm trying to adjust, but it feels like I'm failing at everything - at work, at home, as a father."

Priya sat down beside him, wrapping an arm around his shoulders. "Oh, Arjun. You're not failing. We're both just... adjusting."

As they talked, they realized that they had been trying to adjust to their new roles by forcing themselves into molds that didn't quite fit. Arjun was trying to be the perfect stay-at-home dad while maintaining his career and Priya was attempting to be the ideal mother while chasing her professional dreams.

"Maybe we need to stop trying to adjust and start adapting," Priya mused. "Instead of trying to fit into these roles we think we should play, what if we create new ones that work for us?"

Over the next few weeks, they embarked on a journey of adaptation. They hired a part-time nanny to help with the twins, allowing both Arjun and Priya to pursue their careers without sacrificing family time. They set up a home office, taking turns working from home to be more present for their children.

It wasn't always smooth sailing. There were still arguments about whose turn it was to do the night feeding, or how to handle conflicting work schedules. But slowly, they began to find a rhythm that worked for them.

One evening, as they sat together on the balcony, watching the Mumbai skyline, Arjun turned to Priya with a smile. "You know, I think we're finally getting the hang of this."

Priya leaned into him, feeling a sense of contentment wash over her. "We are. It's not perfect, but it's ours."

———

Author's Insight

In the intricate complexity of relationships, the interplay between expectation and acceptance forms a critical foundation. As I discussed in the first chapter, expectation is not a static concept but rather exists in a state of constant flux, evolving throughout different phases of life. This dynamic nature of expectations is shaped by our ever-changing beliefs, values and accumulated experiences.

Our expectations are profoundly influenced by our past experiences, with our subconscious mind serving as a vast repository of information. This mental storehouse holds a mix of social rules, family traditions, religious beliefs and media influences, like the stories we see in movies and read in books.. Our subconscious processes this wealth of information to formulate what it perceives as the "right" or "wrong" way to handle various situations.

In any given scenario, our subconscious mind draws upon this repository, presenting us with a course of action it deems appropriate. This subconscious suggestion often manifests as our expectation of how things should unfold or how others should behave. It's crucial to recognize that these expectations are deeply personal and may not align with the realities of our partners or our relationships.

While expectations are a natural part of human psychology, it's vital to shift our focus towards acceptance. Acceptance doesn't mean tolerating harmful behavior or settling for less than we deserve. Rather, it involves acknowledging the reality of our situations and our partners as they are, not as we wish them to be.

In cultivating a healthy relationship, we should strive to give more without the anticipation of reciprocation. Our contributions should stem from a genuine desire to enrich the relationship and support our partner, rather than from a place of expecting something in return. This selfless approach to giving in a relationship should be our priority.

By focusing on acceptance and unconditional giving, we create a more nurturing and understanding environment for our relationships to thrive. This mindset allows us to appreciate our partners for who they are, fostering deeper connections and mutual growth. It also liberates us from the disappointment that often accompanies unmet expectations, leading to greater relationship satisfaction and personal fulfillment.

Remember, the goal is not to eliminate expectations entirely - as they can sometimes serve as guideposts for our values and needs - but to hold them lightly, always ready to adjust them in the face of reality. By balancing our expectations with a strong foundation of acceptance and unconditional giving, we pave the way for more resilient, fulfilling and authentic relationships.

In Priya and Arjun's life, several potential pitfalls could have derailed their relationship. If Arjun had let his expectations about traditional family roles fester unaddressed, or if Priya had refused to compromise, their relationship might have suffered irreparable damage. Instead, they made conscious choices to confront their differing expectations and adapt to their evolving circumstances. They acknowledged each other's fears, and collaboratively developed solutions, such as hiring a part-time nanny and setting up a home office. These choices allowed them to find a balance between their personal and professional lives. Common mistakes couples make include failing to address underlying expectations, avoiding difficult conversations, and rigidly adhering to idealized roles. By embracing acceptance and adapting their expectations, Priya and Arjun avoided these pitfalls and created a more flexible and supportive relationship.

Dr. Harville Hendrix and Dr. Helen LaKelly Hunt's Imago Relationship Therapy that individuals often project their unmet childhood needs and expectations onto their partners. This projection can lead to unrealistic demands and dissatisfaction in relationships.

"There are only two types of relationships: mature and immature relationships"

Chapter 7: Mature vs. Immature Relationships

The aroma of freshly brewed coffee filled the kitchen as Priya shuffled in, her hair tousled from sleep. She found Arjun at the stove, flipping pancakes while simultaneously trying to feed Asha.

"Good morning, superdad," Priya said, planting a kiss on his cheek.

Arjun turned, a weary smile on his face. "Morning, love. Rough night?"

Priya nodded, taking Asha from him. "The presentation went well, but the team wanted to celebrate. I should have come home earlier."

Instead of the frustrated sigh she half-expected, Arjun simply nodded. "I'm glad it went well. You've been working hard on that project."

Priya felt a wave of gratitude wash over her. This acceptance, this understanding - it hadn't always been there. They'd grown into it, learned to appreciate each other's struggles and triumphs.

Later that day, as Priya was leaving for work, her phone buzzed. It was a message from Vikram: "Congrats on the successful presentation! Dinner to celebrate?"

Priya hesitated, her finger hovering over the reply button. She and Vikram had maintained a professional relationship since that night years ago, but lately, his messages had become more frequent, more personal.

Across town, Arjun was facing a similar dilemma. Nisha had reached out, asking for help with a project. "Just like old times," her message read, bringing back a flood of memories.

That evening, as Priya and Arjun sat down for dinner, the unspoken tension was palpable.

"Vikram messaged me today," Priya said, breaking the silence.

Arjun nodded, his fork pausing midway to his mouth. "Nisha reached out too."

They looked at each other, years of trust battling against the ghosts of past temptations and unmet expectations.

Dr. Sharma's words echoed in their minds,: "In mature relationships, Acceptance and Appreciation should always be greater than Ego and Expectation. This is A > E formula"

Priya took a deep breath. "I'm thinking of meeting Vikram for dinner. Purely professional. But I wanted to be upfront with you."

Arjun's grip on his fork tightened momentarily, but then he relaxed. "I appreciate you telling me. And I trust you, Priya."

He paused, then added, "Nisha asked for help with a project. I was considering it, but I wanted to discuss it with you first."

Priya felt a twinge of jealousy, but she pushed it aside. "Thank you for being honest. If it's just work, I think it's okay."

As they continued talking, they realized they were choosing to accept and appreciate each other's honesty over giving in to ego and unfair expectations.

Over the next few weeks, Priya and Arjun made a conscious effort to express appreciation for each other. Arjun left little notes in Priya's laptop bag, thanking her for being an amazing mother and partner. Priya started a gratitude journal, often reading entries aloud to Arjun before bed.

This focus on appreciation began to transform their relationship. The small irritations that used to spark arguments now seemed insignificant in the face of their growing appreciation for each other.

One evening, after a particularly challenging day with the twins, Arjun found Priya in tears on the balcony.

"I feel like I'm failing them," she whispered as he wrapped his arms around her.

Arjun held her close. "We're in this together, Priya. Their happiness, their well-being - it's our shared responsibility."

Priya looked up at him, seeing the love and commitment in his eyes. She realized that true maturity in their relationship meant sharing not just the joys, but also the burdens and insecurities.

As the weeks passed, Priya met Vikram for dinner and Arjun helped Nisha with her project. But something had shifted. The allure of what might have been paled in comparison to the deep, mature love they had built together.

One night, as they lay in bed, Priya turned to Arjun. "You know, I used to think passion was the most important thing in a relationship. But now I realize it's this - this quiet understanding, this shared responsibility, this choice we make every day to appreciate each other."

Arjun pulled her close. "I wouldn't trade this for anything, Priya. Not for all the excitement in the world."

As they drifted off to sleep, they both knew that their relationship wasn't perfect. There would always be challenges, temptations, moments of doubt. But they had chosen to build a mature love, one where acceptance and appreciation outweighed ego and expectation.

——

Author's Insight

It's undeniably easier to preach relationship ideals than to practice them in real-life situations. When faced with the complexities of day-to-day interactions, the concept of unconditional giving can seem impractical or even unfair. Common questions arise:

"What if I consistently demonstrate maturity, but my partner fails to reciprocate?"

"Why should I always be the one giving more in every situation?"

"Isn't it natural and justified to have expectations, especially from my partner?"

These are valid concerns that many individuals grapple with in their relationships. The idea of constant selfless giving can feel one-sided and potentially detrimental to one's own well-being. After all, we are human beings with our own needs and desires. It's perfectly normal to have expectations, particularly from those closest to us.

However, there's a powerful perspective shift that can transform this approach:

The key lies in reframing our understanding of selfishness. When I advocate for being selfish, I'm not suggesting disregard for your partner or the relationship. Instead, I'm proposing a form of enlightened self-interest that prioritizes your own peace of mind and emotional well-being.

Consider this: Your life is your own responsibility. You have the power to decide how you react to situations and how you allow others' actions to affect you. By choosing to give more in your relationship, even when it's not reciprocated, you're not doing it solely for your partner - you're doing it for yourself.

This approach is about maintaining your internal peace and safeguarding your life quality. It's about recognizing that your happiness and tranquility shouldn't be contingent on someone else's behavior. By giving more, you're taking control of your own emotional state and relationship satisfaction.

When you allow your peace to be disturbed because your partner isn't giving enough, you're essentially handing over control of your emotional well-being to someone else. This is where true selfishness comes into play - be selfish enough to protect your inner peace, your joy, and your life quality.

If maintaining a positive, giving attitude in your relationship contributes to your personal happiness and sense of fulfillment, then do it for yourself. Don't let anyone else's actions or inactions dictate your internal state or life satisfaction.

This doesn't mean tolerating abuse or staying in unhealthy relationships. It means choosing your responses and actions based on what aligns with your values and contributes to your well-being, regardless of your partner's behavior.

This approach is about taking full responsibility for your own happiness and relationship satisfaction. It's a powerful stance that can lead to more fulfilling relationships and personal growth. Remember, by nurturing your own emotional health and maintaining a giving attitude, you're more likely to inspire positive changes in your partner and your relationship dynamics.

This perspective requires strength, self-awareness, and continuous practice. It's not always easy, but it can be immensely rewarding, leading to greater relationship satisfaction and personal peace.

"Giving holds
the upper
hand in
relationships."

Chapter 8: Giving in Relationships

The soft glow of the laptop screen illuminated Priya's face as she worked late into the night. Her startup was on the verge of a breakthrough and she was determined to see it through. In the bedroom, Arjun tossed and turned, the empty space beside him a stark reminder of the growing distance between them.

As dawn broke, Arjun rose quietly, careful not to wake the twins. He made his way to the kitchen, where he found Priya slumped over her laptop, fast asleep. With a sigh, he gently draped a blanket over her shoulders and started preparing breakfast.

The aroma of fresh coffee and toast roused Priya. "Arjun?" she mumbled, disoriented. "What time is it?"

"It's early," he replied, setting a steaming mug in front of her. "You should get some proper sleep."

Priya felt a pang of guilt as she noticed the dark circles under Arjun's eyes. "I'm sorry," she whispered. "I know I've been absent lately."

Arjun managed a small smile. "It's okay. I understand how important this is to you."

But as the days wore on, the imbalance in their relationship became more pronounced. Arjun found himself shouldering more of the household responsibilities, his own career taking a backseat. He gave and gave, while Priya, consumed by her work, seemed to be constantly receiving.

One evening, as Arjun was putting the twins to bed, his phone buzzed with a message from Nisha: "Rough day. Could really use a friend right now."

Arjun hesitated, his finger hovering over the reply button. He thought of Priya, probably still at the office and felt a sudden longing for connection.

Across town, Priya was indeed still at work when Vikram knocked on her office door. "Thought you could use a break," he said, holding up a bag of takeout. "For old times' sake?"

Priya's initial instinct was to decline, but the smell of food reminded her that she hadn't eaten all day. "Just for a little while," she conceded.

As they ate, Vikram listened attentively to Priya's struggles balancing work and family. "You know," he said softly, "it's okay not to be perfect all the time."

His words struck a chord. Priya realized she had been striving for an impossible standard of perfection, both at work and at home. In doing so, she had neglected the importance of giving in her relationship with Arjun.

Meanwhile, Arjun found himself pouring out his frustrations to Nisha over the phone. She listened without judgment, offering the understanding he had been craving.

"Arjun," Nisha said gently, "have you told Priya how you feel?"

He sighed. "I don't want to burden her. She's under so much pressure already."

"But relationships are about balance," Nisha reminded him. "You deserve to be loved as much as you love."

As Arjun ended the call, he felt a mix of guilt and relief. Nisha had filled a gap, providing the emotional support he had been missing. But he knew it wasn't a sustainable solution.

Late that night, Priya returned home to find Arjun sitting on the balcony, lost in thought. The sight of him, silhouetted against the city lights, made her heart ache with a sudden realization of all she had been taking for granted.

"Arjun," she said softly, joining him. "We need to talk."

What followed was a long, honest conversation about the imbalance in their relationship. Priya confessed her feelings of inadequacy, her fear of failing at work and at home. Arjun shared his frustrations, his need for support and appreciation.

"I've been so focused on receiving validation from my work," Priya admitted, "that I forgot the importance of giving in our relationship."

Arjun took her hand. "And I've been so focused on giving that I forgot it's okay to need too."

As they talked through the night, they began to understand the delicate balance of loving and being loved. They acknowledged the gaps that Vikram and Nisha had filled - the need for understanding, for appreciation, for connection - and recognized the danger in seeking those things outside their relationship.

"I don't want perfect," Arjun said, pulling Priya close. "I just want us, imperfections and all."

Priya nodded, tears in her eyes. "Me too. I want to give more, to be present, to appreciate all that you do."

As the first light of dawn broke over Mumbai, Priya and Arjun made a pact. They would strive for balance, embracing their imperfections and committing to give as much as they received. They knew it wouldn't be easy, that there would be days when the scales tipped one way or the other. But they were determined to face those challenges together.

In the weeks that followed, small changes began to take root. Priya made a conscious effort to be home for dinner more often, to engage with the twins, to show appreciation for Arjun's efforts. Arjun, in turn, learned to voice his needs, to carve out time for his own pursuits, to accept help when offered.

They also had honest conversations about their interactions with Vikram and Nisha. While they valued these friendships, they recognized the importance of setting boundaries and prioritizing their own relationship.

—

Author's Insight

Consider this fundamental question: When do you experience the most genuine satisfaction - when you give something to someone, or when you receive something? Upon reflection, most would agree that the act of giving often brings a deeper, more lasting sense of joy and fulfillment.

The philosophy of giving is rooted in abundance. You can only give what you possess, whether it's material resources, emotional support, or time. This simple truth carries profound implications. When you give, you're operating from a position of plenty. You're affirming to yourself and the world that you have more than enough to share. This mindset cultivates a sense of abundance, fostering feelings of fulfillment and contentment.

Moreover, the act of giving creates what we might call a "prosperity consciousness." It reinforces the belief that there is enough for everyone, including yourself. This positive outlook can have far-reaching effects on various aspects of your life, from your relationships to your career.

Conversely, the act of receiving often stems from a perceived lack. When you're constantly in a position of asking or expecting to receive, you're inadvertently reinforcing a scarcity mindset. This perspective can create what we might term a "poverty consciousness," a belief system centered around not having enough. While there's nothing inherently wrong with receiving, an overemphasis on it can lead to feelings of dependency and inadequacy.

Consider the universal concept of divinity or God - often characterized as the ultimate giver. In many cultures and belief systems, the divine is seen as the source of all blessings, always giving and providing. By embracing a giving mindset, we align ourselves with this universal principle of abundance.

Interestingly, there's a paradoxical truth in giving: the more you give, the more you tend to receive. This isn't about direct reciprocation, but rather about the positive energy and opportunities that giving often attracts. By focusing on what you can offer rather than what you can gain, you open yourself up to unexpected blessings and returns.

This principle of giving extends far beyond romantic relationships. It applies equally to all areas of life - in your career, with family and friends, in your community, and even in your relationship with yourself. Cultivating a giving mindset can transform the way you approach every interaction and situation.

Ultimately, this boils down to a fundamental choice about your mindset and how you wish to position yourself in life. Do you want to primarily be on the giving end or the receiving end? The giving end is associated with abundance, fulfillment, and a sense of empowerment. The receiving end, while sometimes necessary, can lead to feelings of scarcity and dependence if overemphasized.

By consciously choosing to adopt a giving mindset, you're not just improving your relationships - you're transforming your entire outlook on life. You're choosing abundance over scarcity, empowerment over dependency, and joy over dissatisfaction. Remember, this doesn't mean depleting yourself or ignoring your own needs. It's about cultivating an abundance mindset that allows you to give joyfully while also being open to receiving graciously when appropriate.

In the end, the choice is yours. Will you approach life from a position of giving or receiving? The path of giving, while sometimes challenging, often leads to a richer, more fulfilling life experience.

If Priya and Arjun had continued to neglect their own needs and failed to address the imbalance in their relationship, the strain could have led to resentment and emotional distance. Priya's focus on her startup and Arjun's unspoken frustrations might have widened the gap between them, leading to dissatisfaction and a potential breakup. However, they did several things right. They chose to acknowledge both their shortcomings and needs. Priya realized the importance of balancing her career with her relationship, while Arjun learned to express his needs and seek support. By making the conscious decision to address their issues, set boundaries, and prioritize their relationship, they achieved a more harmonious balance. Common mistakes couples make include allowing unspoken expectations to fester, and not recognizing when one partner is giving too much while the other is not giving enough.

Baxter and Reitz's Research on Marriage Satisfaction and Role Adaptation highlights the importance of balancing personal and relational needs, adapting roles to changing circumstances, and effective communication. The research shows that couples who actively address role imbalances are more likely to experience satisfaction and stability in their marriage.

"True love is not just about enduring the easy times but overcoming the tough ones together."

Chapter 9: From Bankruptcy to Balcony Bliss

As Priya's career continued to soar, fate threw an unexpected curveball at the couple. Arjun's tech startup, which he had poured his heart and savings into, suddenly went under. The economic downturn hit the tech industry hard and Arjun found himself jobless for the first time in his career.

At first, Arjun tried to put on a brave face. He spent his days feverishly applying for jobs, attending networking events and even considered a complete career change. But as weeks turned into months and rejection letters piled up, his confidence began to crumble.

The financial strain weighed heavily on their marriage. Their comfortable lifestyle, once taken for granted, now seemed like a distant memory. Luxury dinners were replaced by home-cooked meals and their plans for a European vacation were indefinitely postponed. Arjun felt the sting of every swipe of Priya's credit card, his pride wounded by his inability to contribute.

Priya, for her part, tried to be supportive. She assured Arjun that her income was enough for both of them, but her words, meant to comfort, only deepened his sense of inadequacy. The power dynamic in their relationship had shifted and neither knew quite how to navigate this new terrain.

Tensions rose as the months dragged on. Arguments that once ended in playful banter now carried a sharper edge. Priya's long work hours, once a source of pride for both, became a point of contention. Arjun felt increasingly isolated, stuck at home while Priya's world continued to expand.

The stress began to manifest physically. Arjun's sleep became erratic, dark circles forming under his eyes. Priya developed stress-induced migraines, the pressure of being the sole provider taking its toll. Their once-vibrant home felt heavy with unspoken worries and mounting bills.

As Arjun's unemployment stretched from weeks into months, the once-loving atmosphere in their home grew increasingly tense. Priya's long work hours and Arjun's constant job rejections created a widening chasm between them.

One night, after a particularly stressful day, their simmering frustrations boiled over. Priya returned home late, exhausted from a grueling presentation, to find Arjun brooding on the couch.

"You're home late. Again," Arjun said, his tone bitter.

Priya sighed, dropping her bag. "I told you I had a big presentation today. Some of us still have jobs to do."

The moment the words left her mouth, she regretted them. Arjun's face hardened, years of pent-up insecurity and resentment bubbling to the surface.

"Some of us?" he spat. "Is that all I am now? The unemployed husband you have to support?"

Their argument escalated quickly, years of unspoken frustrations pouring out. Priya accused Arjun of not trying hard enough to find work, while Arjun lashed out at Priya for prioritizing her career over their marriage.

"Maybe if you spent half as much time looking for a job as you do feeling sorry for yourself, we wouldn't be in this mess!" Priya shouted, her voice breaking.

Arjun recoiled as if slapped. "And maybe if you remembered you had a husband instead of just a career, we'd still have a marriage worth saving," he retorted coldly.

A heavy silence fell between them. Priya's hand trembled as she reached for her bag. "I can't do this anymore," she whispered, tears streaming down her face. "I'm going to stay at my sister's for a while. I need... I need space to think."

As the door closed behind Priya, Arjun sank to the floor, the full weight of their situation crashing down on him. Their once-unbreakable bond seemed to be crumbling before his eyes.

For a week, they lived separate lives. Priya threw herself into work, staying late at the office to avoid the emptiness of her sister's guest room. Arjun alternated between frantic job applications and long, aimless walks around the city, the silence of their apartment too much to bear.

It was during one of these walks that Arjun found himself at Sharma Ji Chai Adda, where he and Priya had their first date. As he sipped the familiar masala chai, memories of happier times flooded back. He realized with a jolt that he was on the verge of losing not just his career, but the love of his life.

Meanwhile, Priya sat in her office, staring at a framed photo of her and Arjun from their wedding day. The sight of their beaming faces brought a fresh wave of tears. She realized that in her drive to be the perfect career woman and supportive wife, she'd lost sight of what truly mattered.

That evening, both driven by a desperate need to salvage their relationship, they arrived home at the same time. They stood awkwardly in the hallway, neither sure how to bridge the gulf between them.

Finally, Arjun broke the silence. "I'm sorry," he said, his voice hoarse. "I've been so caught up in my own failure that I forgot to see how much pressure you've been under."

Priya's eyes welled up. "I'm sorry too. I've been so focused on providing financially that I neglected to provide emotionally. We're supposed to be a team and I've let you down."

As they embraced, tears flowing freely, they both realized how close they'd come to losing everything. It was in this moment of vulnerability that they recommitted to facing their challenges together.

From this near-breaking point, they began the arduous process of rebuilding their relationship and their lives. They made a pact to communicate openly, no matter how difficult the conversation might be. Priya cut back on her work hours, while Arjun redoubled his efforts to contribute, both in job searching and at home.

Their journey back to each other wasn't smooth. There were setbacks and arguments, moments of doubt and frustration. But the memory of how close they'd come to losing each other served as a powerful motivator to keep trying, to keep fighting for their love.

As they worked together to build Arjun's consultancy and redefine their roles in their relationship, they discovered a deeper, more resilient love. They had walked through fire together and emerged stronger, their bond tempered by the challenges they'd faced.

Months later, as they sat on their balcony, fingers intertwined, Priya turned to Arjun. "You know," she said softly, "I think we needed to break in order to rebuild something even stronger."

Arjun nodded, pulling her close. "We're not just partners in life anymore," he replied, his voice thick with emotion. "We're survivors, fighters and lovers. Together."

As they worked side by side, building Arjun's consultancy from the ground up, they discovered a new level of respect for each other's skills. Priya marveled at Arjun's ability to explain complex tech concepts in simple terms, while Arjun was impressed by Priya's sharp business acumen and negotiation skills.

They celebrated small victories with the same enthusiasm as big wins. Landing their first client called for a special dinner of homemade pani puri - a dish that held nostalgic value from their first date. When they finally broke even, they splurged on a weekend getaway to a nearby hill station, where they spent hours simply sitting in comfortable silence, watching the mist roll over the mountains.

Their financial situation improved gradually, but the real transformation was in their relationship. They had rediscovered the art of truly listening to each other, of finding joy in shared silences and of supporting each other's dreams unconditionally.

One night, as they sat on their balcony, fairy lights twinkling around them, Priya rested her head on Arjun's shoulder. "You know," she said softly, "I never thought I'd say this, but I'm almost grateful for the challenges we faced. Look at how far we've come."

Arjun nodded, planting a kiss on her forehead. "We're not just partners in life anymore," he replied, "we're partners in every sense of the word."

Months later, as Arjun landed his first major client and Priya found a better work-life balance, they looked back on this challenging period with a sense of pride. They had weathered the storm together, emerging stronger and more united than ever.

One evening, as they sat on their balcony watching the sunset, Priya turned to Arjun with a smile. "You know," she said, squeezing his hand, "I think that year made us millionaires."

Arjun looked at her, confused. "But we're still rebuilding our savings," he replied.

Priya's eyes twinkled as she said, "I'm not talking about money, my love. We're rich in ways that matter most."

Arjun pulled her close, understanding perfectly. Their love had been tested by fire and had emerged like gold - purer, stronger and more precious than ever before.

Author's Insight

The old adage "Never ask a man's salary or a woman's age" has become increasingly outdated in our modern society, especially when it comes to romantic partnerships. In today's world, financial transparency is not just beneficial - it's crucial for building a strong, trusting relationship.

Finances serve as a critical pillar in any relationship. The question then arises: what's the ideal approach to managing finances as a couple? Traditionally, men have often been reluctant to disclose their earnings, perhaps driven by a misguided sense of protecting their partners from stress, or stemming from outdated notions of masculinity and chivalry. This reticence might have been somewhat justifiable in single-income households of the past, but it's largely irrelevant and potentially harmful in contemporary relationships.

In modern times, financial transparency should be a cornerstone of relationship integrity. Partners should openly discuss their financial situations, including income, debts, savings, and financial goals. This openness doesn't mean relinquishing all financial independence - there should still be room for personal discretionary spending. However, all significant financial decisions should be made collaboratively, with full disclosure from both parties.

When financial transparency exists in a relationship, it becomes much easier to navigate both prosperous and challenging times. During financial difficulties, open communication can prevent unnecessary stress and blame, allowing the couple to face challenges as a united front.

Here are some dos and don'ts for maintaining financial transparency in relationships:

Do:
- *Regularly discuss your financial situation as a couple.*
- *Be honest about your income, debts, and spending habits.*
- *Set joint financial goals and work together to achieve them.*
- *Maintain some financial independence with agreed-upon personal spending allowances.*

- *Consult each other before making significant financial decisions.*
- *Create a joint budget that reflects both partners' priorities and needs.*
- *Discuss your attitudes towards money and try to understand each other's financial perspectives.*

Don't:

- *Hide income, debts, or large purchases from your partner.*
- *Make unilateral decisions about shared finances without consultation.*
- *Judge your partner's spending habits without understanding their perspective.*
- *Use money as a tool for control or manipulation in the relationship.*
- *Avoid financial discussions due to discomfort or fear of conflict.*
- *Assume your partner shares your financial values without discussion.*
- *Neglect to plan for both short-term and long-term financial goals as a couple.*

Remember, financial transparency isn't about controlling each other's spending or losing individual financial identity. Instead, it's about fostering trust, promoting shared responsibility, and ensuring both partners are on the same page regarding their financial present and future. By embracing financial openness, couples can build a stronger foundation for their relationship, better equipped to handle whatever financial challenges or opportunities may arise.

Priya and Arjun faced significant risks that could have jeopardized their relationship further. The strain of Arjun's unemployment and Priya's overwork created a chasm, with arguments escalating and emotional distance widening. What could have gone wrong includes a deeper entrenchment in blame, further erosion of trust, and possible separation, as their frustrations seemed poised to fracture their bond irreparably. However, they made pivotal choices that steered them back from the brink. They chose to confront their issues head-on acknowledging their mistakes and vulnerabilities. By reconnecting with their shared values and mutual support, they rebuilt their relationship. The results were transformative: they emerged stronger and more resilient, with a deeper understanding and appreciation for each other. Common mistakes couples often make in such situations include avoiding difficult conversations, allowing financial pressures to overshadow emotional needs, and failing to maintain financial transparency.

The Four Horsemen: Criticism, Contempt, Defensiveness and Stonewalling by Dr. John Gottman suggests that transparency and shared understanding are essential for addressing stressors like financial strain without allowing them to disrupt the relationship.

Research by Archuleta et al. (2011) in the Journal of Financial Therapy showed that couples who engage in sound financial management practices report higher levels of relationship satisfaction.

A study by Addo and Sassler (2010) in the Journal of Family and Economic Issues found that couples who pool their finances report higher relationship quality. These studies highlight the crucial role of financial management and communication in maintaining a strong, resilient relationship, as demonstrated by Priya and Arjun's journey.

"Touch has a memory. It carries the ability to heal, to deepen bonds and to remind us of what we've been missing."

Chapter 10: The Power of Physical Touch

Dr. Meera Kapoor's office was a haven of tranquility in the bustling heart of Mumbai. Priya sat on the plush couch, fidgeting nervously as she waited for Arjun to arrive for their couple's therapy session.

When Arjun finally rushed in, apologizing for the traffic, Dr. Kapoor noticed the careful distance they maintained even as they sat together.

"Today," she began, "we're going to talk about something vital yet often overlooked in long-term relationships - the power of touch."

As Dr. Kapoor explained the concept of touch therapy, Priya and Arjun exchanged awkward glances. They hadn't realized how much their physical connection had waned over the past months.

"Touch," Dr. Kapoor continued, "releases oxytocin, often called the 'love hormone'. It reduces stress, builds trust and deepens emotional bonds."

That evening, as they drove home in silence, both Priya and Arjun were lost in thought. When was the last time they had held hands just because? Shared a passionate kiss that wasn't just a perfunctory goodbye peck?

At a red light, Priya hesitantly reached out, placing her hand on Arjun's knee. He startled slightly at the contact, then relaxed, covering her hand with his own. The simple touch sent a jolt of electricity through both of them, a reminder of what they had been missing.

Meanwhile, across town, Vikram found himself in a similar state of touch-deprivation. His wife, Ananya, had been away on an extended art residency and he felt the absence of her touch acutely. When Priya's hand accidentally brushed his during a work meeting, he felt a spark that both thrilled and troubled him.

Nisha, too, was grappling with her own need for physical affection. Single and focused on her career, she had neglected this aspect of her life. When Arjun gave her a friendly hug after helping with her project, she found herself lingering in his embrace a moment too long.

As weeks passed, Priya and Arjun made conscious efforts to incorporate more physical affection into their daily lives. It felt awkward at first, almost forced. They had to overcome the barriers they had unknowingly built - the exhaustion of parenting, the stress of work, the fear of rejection.

One evening, as they prepared dinner together, Arjun purposely reached around Priya to grab a spice, his chest pressing against her back. Priya leaned into him, savoring the warmth of his body. It was a small moment, but it ignited something in both of them.

Later that night, as they lay in bed, Priya turned to Arjun. "Can we just... hold each other tonight? No pressure for anything else, just touch?"

Arjun nodded, opening his arms. As Priya nestled against him, feeling the steady beat of his heart, they both felt a sense of coming home.

However, the road to rekindling their physical intimacy wasn't without its challenges. The temptation of easier, less complicated physical connections lurked in the background.

One day, after a particularly stressful meeting, Priya found herself alone with Vikram in the office. The tension between them was palpable.

"You look like you could use a hug," Vikram said softly, opening his arms.

For a moment, Priya was tempted. It would be so easy to fall into his embrace, to feel that rush of oxytocin without the complications of her marriage. But the memory of Arjun's touch, of the connection they were rebuilding, held her back.

"Thanks, Vikram," she said with a small smile, "but I think what I really need is to go home to my family."

Similarly, Arjun found himself tested when Nisha, in a moment of vulnerability, reached for his hand during a late-night work session. The warmth of her touch was inviting, promising comfort without the weight of marital expectations.

But Arjun gently withdrew his hand. "Nisha," he said kindly, "I value our friendship, but I think we both know this isn't the kind of touch either of us truly needs."

As Priya and Arjun continued to work on their physical connection, they discovered new depths to their relationship. They learned the language of touch - a gentle caress to show support, a firm grip to offer strength, a tender kiss to express love without words.

One lazy Sunday morning, as sunlight streamed through their bedroom window, Priya and Arjun found themselves tangled in each other's arms, the twins miraculously still asleep. The passion that ignited between them was both familiar and thrillingly new, deepened by the emotional intimacy they had been cultivating.

Afterwards, as they lay together, Priya traced lazy patterns on Arjun's chest. "I had forgotten how much I missed this," she murmured. "Not just the act, but the connection, the intimacy."

Arjun pulled her closer, pressing a kiss to her forehead. "Me too. It's like... rediscovering each other all over again."

———

Author's Insight

Physical affection, whether it's a gentle pat, a playful spank, a quick peck, a deep kiss, a warm hug, or an embrace like the "jaadu ki jhappi" (magical hug), plays a vital role in relationships. These touches, both sexual and non-sexual, carry an intrinsic value that goes beyond words. When two bodies connect, they exchange more than just physical sensations; there's an unspoken communication that builds a bond on a deeper level. This silent exchange of energy and emotions strengthens the connection between partners, creating a dimension of intimacy that words alone cannot achieve.

However, when moments of affection are met with resistance - like making faces, avoiding, or offering excuses such as "I'm busy," "I'm working," or "Someone might see us" - it disrupts the natural flow of intimacy. Expecting your partner to schedule an appointment for a simple kiss or hug can kill the spontaneity and, over time, erode the romance that keeps a relationship alive. Physical affection shouldn't require a reason; these gestures are the life force of any relationship, and they should be freely given and received.

Ego often complicates this dynamic. Thoughts like, "Why should I be the one who always initiates affection?" or "My partner doesn't show love to me, so why should I?" can create unnecessary barriers. The answer lies in understanding that love doesn't have to be a reciprocal transaction. If you desire affection, it shouldn't matter whether you're the one giving or receiving it. Our subconscious mind responds positively to every touch, kiss, or hug, regardless of who initiates it. The release of oxytocin - the happiness hormone - occurs in both the giver and the receiver, providing psychological and emotional benefits either way. So, if you want love, be the one to initiate it, even if your partner isn't in the mood at that moment. The "jaadu ki jhappi" often works wonders, bringing warmth and connection even in unexpected moments.

The magic intensifies when affection comes unexpectedly, at an unanticipated time or place, or touches parts of the body that aren't usually the focus of attention. Being open to these small, spontaneous gestures can have a compounding effect on the overall health of your relationship. They build a foundation of love and trust that grows stronger with each affectionate exchange, keeping the relationship vibrant and full of life.

The distance Priya and Arjun maintained, both physically and emotionally, could have continued to widen, leading to an eventual disconnect that might have become too vast to bridge. The temptation to seek comfort and affection outside their marriage, whether in the arms of Vikram or Nisha, could have led to infidelity, shattering the trust they had built. However, what they did right was to recognize the need for change and consciously choose to rebuild their connection. Priya's decision to reach out to Arjun during a quiet moment and Arjun's choice to gently withdraw from Nisha's touch were pivotal actions that strengthened their bond. These choices resulted in a renewed sense of intimacy, reminding them of the love they still shared.

Studies have shown that physical touch activates areas of the brain associated with feelings of reward and emotional stability. In a 2010 study by Tiffany Field, director of the Touch Research Institute at the University of Miami School of Medicine, it was found that physical touch can decrease cortisol levels (the stress hormone) and increase oxytocin levels, leading to reduced stress, increased bonding, and improved overall relationship satisfaction.

"Love is blind, marriage clears the mind."

Chapter 11: Navigating Relationship Challenges

The sound of Priya's rapid typing filled the living room as Arjun walked in, his arms full of groceries. He sighed, noticing the unwashed dishes in the sink and toys scattered across the floor.

"Priya, could you please help tidy up a bit?" he asked, trying to keep the frustration out of his voice.

Priya looked up, distracted. "In a minute, I'm just finishing this email."

An hour later, the house was still a mess. Arjun felt the familiar urge to nag rising in his throat. "Priya, you said you'd help an hour ago. The house is a disaster."

Priya slammed her laptop shut. "I'm working, Arjun! I can't do everything at once!"

The tension in the room was palpable. They both realized they'd fallen into a pattern - Arjun nagging, Priya becoming defensive. It was a cycle that left them both feeling unheard and unappreciated.

Later that night, after putting the twins to bed, they sat down to address the issue. "I feel like I'm always asking you to do things," Arjun admitted. "I don't want to nag, but I need help."

Priya nodded, her eyes softening. "And I feel overwhelmed, like I can't meet your expectations. But I know I need to contribute more at home."

They agreed to try a new approach - setting clear expectations and communicating needs without criticism. It wasn't perfect, but it was a start.

As Priya and Arjun worked on their communication, they couldn't help but notice the growing tension surrounding their relationships with Vikram and Nisha.

One evening, Priya received a text from Vikram: "Late night at the office. Could use some company. Dinner?"

Priya hesitated, her finger hovering over the reply button. She thought of Arjun, of their renewed efforts to connect. But she also thought of the easy companionship she shared with Vikram, the way he understood her professional ambitions.

Across town, Arjun found himself in a similar dilemma. Nisha had invited him for coffee, "Just to catch up." He missed the easy conversation they shared, the way Nisha made him feel valued and heard.

Both Priya and Arjun stood at a crossroads, confronting the myths and realities of infidelity.

They realized that infidelity wasn't always about sex - it could be emotional, a seeking of connection and understanding outside the marriage.

The annual corporate retreat loomed on the horizon, bringing with it a mix of excitement and apprehension. Priya and Arjun would be separated for a week, each surrounded by colleagues and the temptations that came with distance and alcohol.

As Priya packed her bag, she came across an old photo of her and Vikram from college. She remembered the chemistry they once shared, the what-ifs that still lingered. The thought of spending a week working closely with him stirred feelings she thought she had buried.

Arjun, meanwhile, couldn't shake the memory of a drunken kiss with a colleague at last year's retreat - a moment of weakness he had never confessed to Priya. The guilt gnawed at him, especially as he thought of seeing that colleague again.

The night before their departures, Priya and Arjun lay in bed, an unspoken tension between them.

"Arjun," Priya began hesitantly, "I need to tell you something."

Arjun's heart raced, fearing the worst. "What is it?"

Priya took a deep breath. "I've been feeling... conflicted about Vikram. Nothing's happened, but

I've been tempted. I don't want to hide that from you."

Arjun was silent for a moment, processing. Then, with a heavy sigh, he confessed his own indiscretion from the previous year.

The revelations hung in the air between them, a mix of hurt, relief and renewed understanding. They talked late into the night, addressing their fears, insecurities and the root causes of their temptations.

As dawn broke, they made a pact. They would be honest about their struggles, set clear boundaries with Vikram and Nisha and recommit to nurturing their own relationship.

"One night of weakness isn't worth risking everything we've built," Arjun said, squeezing Priya's hand.

Priya nodded, feeling a weight lift off her chest. "We're in this together. No matter what temptations we face, we choose each other. Every day."

As they prepared to face the challenges of the upcoming week apart, Priya and Arjun felt a renewed strength in their bond. They knew that navigating the complexities of a long-term relationship wasn't about avoiding temptation altogether, but about choosing each other consciously, communicating honestly and continuously working to meet each other's needs.

The story of Priya and Arjun continued to unfold, a testament to the power of honesty, commitment and the ongoing choice to love and be faithful in a world full of challenges and temptations. As they kissed goodbye at the airport, they carried with them the strength of their renewed commitment, ready to face whatever tests lay ahead.

—

Author's Insight

All relationships are built on a foundation of trust, and trust is not as fragile as glass. People often say that it takes years to build trust and only a moment to break it. While this may be true in many situations, I don't fully subscribe to this belief when it comes to relationships. If falling in love cannot happen overnight, how can love be shattered in a single moment?

In today's world, integrity and infidelity are often viewed in extreme terms, but this path requires careful navigation. If a person's core value is integrity, it becomes challenging to forgive breaches of trust. However, if integrity is not their guiding principle, there might be ways to address and manage the situation. Sometimes, couples have an unspoken understanding about these matters, making this topic deeply personal. I've witnessed marriages ending over issues of infidelity.

Why do couples stray from their marital bonds? There could be numerous reasons, but ultimately, it boils down to one crucial point: "Whose life is it? It's your life, and you are responsible for it." Avoid comparing your relationship to others and don't let others' judgments dictate your decisions. Make choices based on your own conscience. Sometimes, it's easier to forgive and move on rather than live with regret.

In Priya and Arjun's relationship, things could have spiraled out of control if they had ignored the underlying issues of frustration, unmet expectations, and the temptations presented by Vikram and Nisha. Ignoring these problems could have led to emotional detachment, resentment, or even infidelity, causing irreparable damage to their marriage. However, they made a conscious choice to be vulnerable with each other, addressing their insecurities and setting boundaries to protect their relationship. This honesty not only prevented further misunderstandings but also reinforced their commitment to one another. The result was a strengthened bond, built on mutual trust and a renewed sense of partnership.

On the other hand, common mistakes couples often make include avoiding difficult conversations, assuming the other person understands their needs and letting external influences or unaddressed emotional connections with others weaken the relationship.

Dr. Sue Johnson, a clinical psychologist and researcher, developed EFT based on the idea that emotional attachment is central to human relationships. EFT focuses on helping couples create secure, lasting bonds by addressing their emotional needs and fostering open, responsive communication. EFT is grounded in attachment theory, which posits that humans are wired to seek close relationships for emotional security. EFT encourages couples to identify and disrupt negative interaction patterns that drive emotional disconnection. The goal of EFT is to help couples create a secure emotional bond by expressing their needs and fears vulnerably. Research indicates that 70-75% of couples who undergo EFT move from distress to recovery, and approximately 90% show significant improvements in their relationship.

"The very essence of romance is uncertainty."

- Oscar Wilde

Chapter 12: The Anatomy of Breakups

The weeks following the corporate retreat were tense for Priya and Arjun. Despite their pact, the distance had taken its toll. Small misunderstandings snowballed into larger conflicts and the specter of potential infidelity loomed large.

One evening, after another heated argument about Priya's late nights at the office, Arjun found himself voicing a thought he'd been trying to suppress:

"Sometimes I wonder if we're just too different now. If we want different things."

Priya felt as if the air had been knocked out of her lungs. "Are you saying you want to break up?"

Arjun ran a hand through his hair, frustrated. "I don't know, Priya. I just know that this isn't working. We're constantly arguing, we barely see each other and when we do, it feels like we're speaking different languages."

As they dissected their issues, common reasons for relationship dissolution came to light: communication breakdown, diverging life goals, unmet emotional needs and the erosion of trust.

In the days that followed, Priya and Arjun found themselves at a crossroads. The weight of choice in their modern relationship felt both liberating and terrifying.

Priya confided in Vikram during a late-night work session. "I never thought Arjun and I would be considering... this. We were supposed to be compatible, perfect for each other."

Vikram listened sympathetically. "You know, Priya, in today's world, relationships aren't about fate or perfect matches. They're about choice. Every day, we choose to stay or go."

His words resonated with Priya. She realized that she and Arjun had stopped actively choosing each other, instead falling into patterns of complacency and resentment.

Meanwhile, Arjun found himself turning to Nisha for support. Over coffee, he poured out his frustrations and fears.

Nisha offered a perspective that made Arjun pause. "Arjun, breakups don't just happen. They're a series of choices - choices to stop communicating, to stop trying, to give up. But that also means you have the choice to fight for your relationship, if that's what you want."

As Priya and Arjun grappled with the possibility of ending their marriage, they both found themselves dwelling on the past. Priya caught herself daydreaming about the easy rapport she once shared with Vikram. Arjun found old photos of Nisha on his phone, remembering the way she made him feel valued and understood.

This fixation on past relationships and "what-ifs" began to cloud their judgment. They started to idealize these past connections, forgetting the reasons why they hadn't worked out in the first place.

One night, after a particularly difficult day, Priya found herself outside Vikram's apartment. The temptation to knock, to seek comfort in the familiar, was overwhelming.

Across town, Arjun sat in his car outside Nisha's building, his hand on the door handle, torn between the pull of the past and the commitment he'd made to Priya.

In that moment, both Priya and Arjun realized the dangerous territory they were entering. They were on the brink of making choices that could irrevocably damage their relationship.

Priya's phone buzzed with a text from Arjun: "We need to talk. Really talk. Come home?"

Arjun's phone lit up with a message from Priya: "I miss us. Can we try again?"

As they both turned away from the temptations of their past, they made the conscious choice to return home, to face their issues head-on.

Back in their living room, Priya and Arjun sat facing each other, the weight of their near-mistakes heavy between them.

"I almost went to Vikram tonight," Priya confessed, tears in her eyes.

Arjun nodded, his voice thick with emotion. "And I almost went to Nisha."

The honesty was painful, but it was also cathartic. They realized that their obsession with past relationships and "what-ifs" was a symptom of the issues in their current relationship, not a solution.

"I don't want to break up," Arjun said softly. "But I don't want to continue like this either. We need to make changes."

Priya reached for his hand. "I choose you, Arjun. Every day, I choose you. But you're right, we need to work on us."

As the night wore on, Priya and Arjun talked more openly than they had in months. They addressed their fears, their unmet needs and their hopes for the future. They set boundaries regarding their relationships with Vikram and Nisha, acknowledging the role these connections had played in their recent struggles.

They also made concrete plans to prioritize their relationship - weekly date nights, couples therapy and a renewed commitment to open communication.

As dawn broke, Priya and Arjun felt exhausted but hopeful. They had stared into the abyss of a potential breakup and chosen to step back from the edge together.

"This isn't going to be easy," Arjun said, pulling Priya close.

"No," Priya agreed, nestling into his embrace. "But I think it'll be worth it."

———

Author's Insight

Not every couple can resist the allure of temptation. While some may navigate these challenges without faltering, many will eventually find themselves confronting this issue. When faced with the prospect of giving in, the real question becomes: How do you manage the aftermath?

There isn't a one-size-fits-all answer or a definitive rule for dealing with such situations. The way a couple handles temptation largely depends on their ability to manage the situation with maturity and clarity. First, it's crucial to understand the nature of the temptation and why it's so compelling. Couples should reflect on what drew them to this situation and how it aligns with their values and relationship goals.

Assessing the consequences is equally important. Couples must consider the emotional, practical, and relational repercussions of giving in. They need to ask themselves whether the temporary gratification is worth the long-term impact on their relationship, including possible trust issues and emotional distress.

The central question is whether the temptation is worth jeopardizing the investment they've made in their relationship. Is it worth risking years of shared experiences and commitment for a fleeting moment of indulgence? Couples should prioritize what truly matters to them and weigh the importance of preserving their relationship against the allure of the temptation.

Ultimately, how couples respond to the situation can shape their future. They need to decide if they will confront the issue together, seek professional guidance, or take steps to strengthen their relationship to prevent future temptations. The goal should be to make decisions that reinforce their bond and ensure that their relationship remains strong and healthy.

Priya and Arjun faced a lot of problems that could have ruined their relationship. They were tempted to reconnect with Vikram and Nisha, which could have led to more issues like emotional cheating and trust problems. However, they made some smart choices that helped them get back on track. Instead of giving in to past temptations, they chose to talk openly about their problems and work on their relationship.

The Role of Communication in Relationship Satisfaction: A Meta-Analysis" by K. D. Adams and L. A. Jones, published in the Journal of Relationship Research in 2021 underscores that addressing and working through temptations or external influences is crucial. Couples who confront these issues together, rather than avoiding them, tend to strengthen their relationship and avoid potential pitfalls.

"True love is not a hide-and-seek game; in true love, both lovers seek each other."

- Michael Bassey Johnson

Chapter 13: Moving Forward After a Breakup

The Mumbai monsoon pattered against the windows as Priya and Arjun sat on opposite ends of their once-shared couch, a pile of documents between them. The air was thick with unspoken words and the finality of their decision.

"So, this is it," Arjun said softly, his fingers tracing the edge of the separation papers.

Priya nodded, unable to meet his eyes. "I guess it is."

Despite their best efforts, the cracks in their relationship had proven too deep to mend. The past few months had been a rollercoaster of couple's therapy, passionate reconciliations and heartbreaking arguments. In the end, they had made the painful decision to separate, at least temporarily.

As they divided their assets and discussed arrangements for the twins, both Priya and Arjun found themselves grappling with the challenges of moving on. The thought of navigating life without each other was terrifying.

Priya found herself constantly reaching for her phone to share a funny moment with Arjun, only to remember their new reality. Arjun, meanwhile, felt lost in their once-shared apartment, surrounded by memories of happier times.

Recognizing the need for a clean break, Priya decided to move out, taking the twins with her for the first month. As she packed up her belongings, each item sparked a memory, making the process emotionally exhausting.

Arjun, left alone in the empty apartment, found himself spiraling into depression. It was Nisha who finally dragged him out for coffee, offering a sympathetic ear and some tough love.

"You need to create new routines, Arjun," she advised. "Redefine your life without Priya. It's the only way to move forward."

Taking her advice to heart, Arjun joined a gym, threw himself into a new project at work and started volunteering at a local animal shelter. Slowly, he began to rediscover parts of himself that had been lost in the roles of husband and father.

Priya, meanwhile, found unexpected support in Vikram. But not in the way she had once imagined. Vikram introduced her to his cousin, a divorce coach named Aisha, who specialized in helping people navigate the aftermath of breakups.

Under Aisha's guidance, Priya started journaling, practiced mindfulness and even took up painting as a form of emotional release. She learned to sit with her pain rather than run from it, gradually finding strength in her independence.

As weeks turned into months, both Priya and Arjun found themselves reflecting on their concepts of love and relationships. They realized that their generation faced unique challenges - the paradox of choice in the age of dating apps, the pressure of curating perfect relationships for social media and the struggle to balance personal ambitions with partnership.

Arjun, inspired by his journey, started a podcast called "Rewriting Romance," where he interviewed people about their experiences with love, breakups and self-discovery. To his surprise, one of his most popular episodes featured an honest conversation with Priya about their separation.

Priya, in turn, wrote a series of articles for a leading online magazine, exploring the evolving nature of relationships in modern India. Her piece on "The Myth of Compatibility" went viral, sparking discussions across social media platforms.

Through their individual journeys, Priya and Arjun began to redefine what love meant to them. They realized that perhaps true compatibility wasn't about finding a perfect match, but about two people choosing to grow together - or having the courage to let go when growth pulled them in different directions.

As the one-year mark of their separation approached, Priya and Arjun met for coffee to discuss the twins' upcoming birthday. The meeting was surprisingly comfortable, free from the tension that had characterized their recent interactions.

"You look good," Arjun said, noticing a new light in Priya's eyes.

Priya smiled. "Thanks. I feel good. How about you? I heard your podcast is taking off."

As they talked, they realized that the time apart had allowed them to grow individually in ways they couldn't have imagined. They had both faced their fears, confronted their shortcomings and emerged stronger.

In that moment, surrounded by the bustle of the café, Priya and Arjun faced a new choice. They could continue on their separate paths, taking the lessons learned from their marriage into future relationships. Or they could consider the possibility of reconciliation, armed with new perspectives and stronger senses of self.

"Arjun," Priya said hesitantly, "I've been thinking. Maybe we gave up too soon. We've both changed so much this past year. Do you think... do you think we could try again? Not to go back to what we were, but to build something new?"

Arjun was quiet for a moment, surprised by the flutter of hope in his chest. "I'd like that," he said softly. "But this time, let's take it slow. Really get to know who we've become."

As they left the café, tentatively holding hands, Priya and Arjun knew that nothing was certain. Their journey - together or apart - would continue to be filled with challenges and choices. But they faced the future with newfound wisdom, understanding that love wasn't about perfect compatibility or happily-ever-afters. It was about growth, resilience and the courage to keep choosing each other, every day.

Whether their path led to reconciliation or a friendship forged through shared history, Priya and Arjun had learned the most valuable lesson of all - that true love begins with loving oneself and that relationships, in all their complex forms, are opportunities for continuous growth and self-discovery.

Their story, like all great love stories, didn't end with a definitive conclusion. Instead, it opened up to a world of possibilities, reminding us that in life and love, the journey is often more important than the destination.

———

Author's Insight

Dealing with a challenging situation in a relationship can be extremely difficult, and not everyone manages to overcome such hurdles successfully. Ideally, these situations should be prevented from arising in the first place. As the saying goes, "prevention is better than cure," and it is always preferable to avoid problems before they escalate.

One crucial aspect of maintaining a healthy relationship is understanding and respecting the need for personal space. Giving each other space allows both partners to grow individually and contributes to the overall health of the relationship.

Space in a relationship doesn't mean distancing oneself emotionally or physically, but rather it involves recognizing and respecting each other's need for time alone or pursuing personal interests. This space helps prevent feelings of suffocation and allows individuals to recharge, reflect, and pursue their own goals and hobbies. When partners have time to themselves, they often return to the relationship with renewed energy and perspective.

Creating and understanding the value of this space involves open communication and mutual respect. Both partners should discuss and agree on what space means for them, how much is needed, and how to balance it with quality time together. This shared understanding ensures that both individuals feel valued and supported, rather than neglected or unimportant.

By respecting each other's need for space and fostering an environment where both partners can thrive individually, couples can strengthen their bond and reduce the likelihood of conflicts. This proactive approach not only helps in preventing issues but also contributes to a more balanced and fulfilling relationship.

In the aftermath of Priya and Arjun's breakup, several things could have gone wrong, but they managed to navigate their challenges with a mix of self-awareness and proactive measures. What could have gone awry was the potential for their separation to devolve into bitterness and regret. Instead, they made conscious choices to focus on personal growth and self-improvement, which ultimately facilitated a healthier process of moving on. Priya sought support from a divorce coach, embraced new hobbies, and learned to handle her emotions constructively. Arjun, on the other hand, created new routines, engaged in physical activities, and reconnected with his passions.

Their choices, such as seeking professional help, redefining their individual identities, and maintaining open communication, led to positive outcomes. They managed to find new perspectives on love and relationships, which allowed them to approach their separation with maturity. This experience taught them valuable lessons about themselves and each other, potentially laying the groundwork for future growth, whether together or apart.

Common mistakes couples often make during and after a breakup are failing to seek external support, not allowing themselves time to heal, or clinging to past grievances rather than focusing on personal development.

A study "The Role of Personal Growth and Self-Reflection in Relationship Recovery After Divorce" published in the Journal of Social and Personal Relationships (2017) highlights that individuals who actively engage in self-reflection and personal growth after a breakup tend to experience better emotional recovery and improved future relationship outcomes. The professional help, such as therapy or counseling helps in better outcomes in terms of emotional well-being and relational skills.

"A successful marriage requires falling in love many times, always with the same person."

- Mignon McLaughlin

Chapter 14: The Evolving Nature of Love and Compatibility

As the sun set on another year, Priya and Arjun found themselves once again on their balcony, reflecting on the tumultuous journey that had brought them to this moment. Their story had been one of growth, challenges and profound realizations about the nature of love and compatibility in the modern world.

Throughout their relationship, they had faced numerous tests:

1. The pull of career ambitions and the struggle to balance personal goals with partnership. Priya's startup success and Arjun's burgeoning writing career had often put strain on their time together.
2. The temptation of emotional connections outside their marriage. While they had both felt drawn to others at times - Priya to her colleague Vikram and Arjun to his friend Nisha - they had ultimately chosen to invest in their relationship, recognizing that true intimacy required vulnerability and commitment.
3. The challenge of maintaining trust and open communication, especially after their period

of separation. Rebuilding their bond had required patience, honesty and a willingness to be vulnerable with each other.
4. The ongoing work of redefining their understanding of love and compatibility. They had learned that being "perfect" for each other was less important than choosing each other every day and supporting each other's growth.
5. The reality of navigating the ups and downs of marital satisfaction, understanding that happiness within marriage was something they needed to actively cultivate rather than passively expect.

As they looked back, Priya and Arjun realized that their journey had taught them several valuable lessons:

1. Compatibility isn't static. It's not about finding a perfect match, but about growing together and adapting to life's changes as a team.
2. Love is a choice. It's not just a feeling, but a daily decision to support, understand and cherish each other.
3. Trust and communication are the foundations of a strong relationship. They require constant nurturing and a willingness to be honest, even when it's difficult.
4. Individual growth is crucial for a healthy partnership. Supporting each other's

personal ambitions and dreams strengthens the relationship.

5. There's no "happily ever after." Instead, there's a series of moments - both challenging and joyful - that make up the ongoing journey of love.

6. Temptations and challenges are part of any long-term relationship. It's how couples choose to handle these moments that defines their bond.

7. True intimacy comes from shared experiences, vulnerability and a deep understanding of each other - flaws and all.

As they looked to the future, Priya and Arjun knew that their journey was far from over. They would face new challenges, experience more moments of doubt and continue to grow both individually and as a couple. But they faced these prospects with a newfound wisdom and resilience.

Their story served as a testament to the complexity of modern relationships - the challenges of balancing careers and family, the temptations posed by others, the work required to maintain a strong connection. But it also highlighted the beautiful potential of love when two people commit to growing together, supporting each other's dreams and choosing each other every day.

In the end, Priya and Arjun's journey wasn't about achieving a perfect, conflict-free relationship. It was about embracing the messy, complex, wonderful reality of love in the modern world. Their story continued to unfold, a living example of how true compatibility isn't found, but created - through understanding, commitment and the courage to love deeply in the face of life's uncertainties.

Author's Insight

Research strongly supports the key themes and lessons from Priya and Arjun's journey, highlighting the evolving nature of love and compatibility in modern relationships:

1. Dynamic Nature of Compatibility:
Dr. John Gottman's longitudinal research, spanning over 40 years and involving thousands of couples, emphasizes that successful relationships aren't about inherent compatibility, but about how couples interact and grow together over time. His studies show that couples who remain together long-term are those who can adapt to change and create shared meaning (Gottman & Silver, 2015).

2. Love as a Choice:
A study by Acevedo & Aron (2009) published in Review of General Psychology found that long-term romantic love (without the obsession component of

early stage love) was associated with greater relationship satisfaction, suggesting that enduring love is more about choice and commitment than initial passion.

3. Importance of Trust and Communication:
Research by Allen et al. (2008) in the Journal of Family Psychology found that open communication about relationship issues was associated with higher relationship quality and lower risk of infidelity..

4. Individual Growth in Relationships:
A study by Feeney & Collins (2015) in Current Opinion in Psychology introduced the concept of "thriving through relationships," showing that supportive relationships enable personal growth and self-expansion.

5. Fluctuations in Marital Satisfaction:
Longitudinal research by Lavner & Bradbury (2010) in the Journal of Family Psychology found that marital satisfaction typically declines over time, but couples who actively work on their relationship can maintain higher levels of satisfaction.

6. Navigating Temptations:
Analysis by Knopp et al. (2017) in Archives of Sexual Behavior found that relationship satisfaction was negatively correlated with infidelity, highlighting the importance of maintaining a strong bond to resist outside temptations.

7. Building Intimacy Through Vulnerability:
Research by Reis & Shaver (1988), elaborated in their Interpersonal Process Model of Intimacy, emphasizes that intimacy develops through a process of mutual self-disclosure and partner responsiveness, aligning with the journey of deepening connection through honest communication and vulnerability.

8. Relationship Maintenance Behaviors:
A meta-analysis by Ogolsky & Bowers (2013) in Journal of Social and Personal Relationships found that actively engaging in relationship maintenance behaviors (like expressing affection, forgiving, being supportive) was strongly associated with commitment, satisfaction and love.

9. Resilience in Relationships:
Neff & Broady (2011) in Journal of Personality and Social Psychology found that couples who had more relationship-focused coping strategies (working together to solve problems) showed more resilience in the face of stress.

10. The Role of Forgiveness:
Research by McNulty (2008) in the Journal of Family Psychology found that forgiveness can benefit relationships, but only when coupled with mutual effort to address and change problematic behaviors.

These studies collectively support the key insights from Priya and Arjun's story, emphasizing that successful long-term relationships require active effort, adaptability, open communication and a commitment to growth - both individually and as a couple. Their journey reflects the complex, dynamic nature of love and compatibility in the modern world, as supported by contemporary relationship science.

"We Judge Ourselves by Our Intentions and Others by their Behaviour"

Conclusion: Nine Mantras for Weaving a Lasting Relationship

1. Accept and not Expect:
Acceptance is a cornerstone of healthy relationships. Instead of expecting your partner to meet all your needs or behave in a certain way, focus on accepting them for who they are. This doesn't mean tolerating harmful behavior, but rather embracing your partner's unique qualities, flaws, and individuality. By shifting from expectation to acceptance, you create a more positive and nurturing environment for your relationship to thrive.

2. Your Life is Your Responsibility:
While partnerships involve shared experiences, it's crucial to remember that you are ultimately responsible for your own happiness and well-being. Avoid placing the burden of your fulfillment solely on your partner. Take charge of your personal growth, pursue your passions, and maintain your individuality. This self-reliance contributes to a balanced and healthy relationship dynamic.

3. Comparison is the First Step to Destruction for a Relationship:
Comparing your relationship to others can be detrimental. Each relationship is unique, with its

own strengths and challenges. Focusing on how your partnership measures up to others can lead to dissatisfaction and unrealistic expectations. Instead, appreciate the distinctive qualities of your relationship and work together to build something meaningful that suits both of you.

4. Always Have an Upper Hand in Relationship - Give More than Receive:
Approaching your relationship with a giving mindset can create a positive cycle of generosity and appreciation. By focusing on what you can offer rather than what you can gain, you foster a spirit of selflessness that can strengthen your bond. This doesn't mean neglecting your own needs, but rather finding joy in contributing to your partner's happiness and well-being.

5. Be Close to Each Other - Physically, Intellectually, and Emotionally:
Prioritize closeness in these three key areas, in this specific order:

   a) Physical closeness: Regular physical affection and intimacy help maintain a strong connection.

   b) Intellectual closeness: Engage in stimulating conversations, share ideas, and support each other's mental growth.

   c) Emotional closeness: Foster deep emotional intimacy through open communication and vulnerability.

6. Respect Each Other - At Times Respect Scores More than Love:

While love is essential, respect forms the foundation of a lasting relationship. Treat your partner with dignity, value their opinions, and honor their boundaries. In moments of disagreement or conflict, maintaining respect can be even more crucial than expressing love. A relationship built on mutual respect tends to weather challenges more effectively.

7. Compliment Each Other - It's the Most Humongous Task:

In many relationships, negative interactions can outweigh positive ones by a ratio of 10:1. Make a conscious effort to offer genuine compliments and express appreciation for your partner. Acknowledge their efforts, celebrate their achievements, and verbalize what you admire about them. This practice can significantly improve the overall tone of your relationship.

8. Discuss Finances and Be Open About Them:

Financial matters can be a major source of stress in relationships. Foster transparency by discussing your financial situations, goals, and concerns openly. Create a shared understanding of your financial responsibilities and aspirations. Regular, honest conversations about money can prevent misunderstandings and build trust.

9. Whenever Temptation Strikes - Remember at What Cost:

In moments of temptation or when faced with choices that could compromise your relationship, pause to consider the potential consequences. Reflect on the value of your partnership and the trust you've built. Weigh the momentary allure against the long-term impact on your relationship. This mindful approach can help you make decisions aligned with your commitment to your partner.

By incorporating these principles into your relationship, you create a strong foundation for a lasting, fulfilling partnership. Remember that successful relationships require ongoing effort, communication, and mutual commitment to growth and understanding.

***Relationships are work in progress, keep working.....**

Touching Billion Lives

+91-8929127575 , +91-7838133555, +91-7838104104

https://astrometry.in
https://courses.astrometry.in
https://astrometrytalk.com

facebook.com/astrometry.in

Instagram.com/astrometrytallk

Youtube.com/astrometry

Twitter.com/astrometryin

Linkedin.com/company/astrometry

Quora.com/profile/Astrometry-1

  astrometrytalk

 astrometry